How to Pick The Best Tenant

By

Carolyn Gibson

This book is a work of non-fiction. Names and places have been changed to protect the privacy of all individuals. The events and situations are true.

ISBN: 1-4107-6625-X (e-book)
ISBN: 1-4107-6626-8 (Paperback)

Library of Congress Control Number: 2003094867

This book is printed on acid free paper.

Printed in the United States of America
Bloomington, IN

1stBooks – rev. 11/24/03

This book is dedicated to the memory of my father
Mose Gibson,
Who managed our three-family home,
And was the first landlord I ever knew.

Best wishes
for your tenant search!
Carolyn Gibson
3/16/05

<u>Acknowledgements</u>

The following friends, relatives, and colleagues provided me with invaluable support, advice, their influence, confidence, information, encouragement, and enthusiasm for my work:

Mary Ellen Gibson, my mother
Elaine Gibson, my sister
Stan Gibson, my brother
Kimberly A. Blair, my niece
Tony V. Blaize, esq.
Valor Breez, Sr.
Hazel Briceno
Robert Flagg
Glenn L. French, CPM®
Ophelia Howe
Charles S. Mancuso, esq.
Alice Sanford

TABLE OF CONTENTS

Why I Wrote This Book

One day I was in the Boston, Massachusetts Housing Court for one of my clients. To my astonishment, I saw several former tenants that I had evicted at one time or another years ago walk through the housing court system again. A few were being evicted for the third time. I asked myself, "How can people who have been evicted two and three times in the same city over a period of years manage to find another apartment?" Even further, in this day of computer technology and the Information Age, "How is it that high-risk tenants can still manage to evade the application processing system, and get an apartment'?

It occurred to me that over my many years of managing residential property, I never had a manual or book specifically geared to help me pick a good tenant. It was a learning experience over time, of trials and errors, of mistakes and lessons learned, teaching and taking seminars, of networking with my fellow managers that helped me to improve at selecting good applicants.

"What about those home owners that do not have the same access to information as I have had and was able to learn for over twenty years?" I asked. "What does the average homeowner, or first time homeowner do to find a good tenant? How can they learn to find the best of the bunch when there is no manual for them to read?" I quickly realized that the only venue for homeowners to learn from were their experiences, good or bad, or word of mouth. They had no real *preventive* way of separating high-risk tenants from anyone else knocking on their door looking for an apartment.

I decided that writing a book about the best ways to take a rental application, verify the information written on it, and how to use some decision making tools to select a tenant would be beneficial to millions of homeowners and managers alike. The techniques outlined in this book will take the guessing out of tenant selection, and will make picking a tenant an information-based process.

Picking the best tenant is never fool proof. An applicant you think is perfect could turn out to be the worst tenant you have selected in years. Another rental applicant you decide to take a chance on may turn out to be one of your best tenants.

Regardless of the city or state location, or the amount of rent charged, there is a renting process that should be standard for every rental applicant. A good tenant makes an owner happy. It also makes the overall tenancy in the apartment easier. Renting a vacant apartment to a responsible person or family is good for real estate financial stability.

This book covers over two decades of my professional experience managing residential property. I have also used these techniques when renting out my personal vacancies. I know from experience and practice that these techniques work best in securing a long term, dependable, rent paying, problem-free tenant.

I have taught the process of renting an apartment to homeowners, students, and managers across the United States. The techniques, suggestions, and recommendations are applicable to renting out single-family houses, two and three family housing, subsidized housing, and multi-family residential complexes. It is my goal that the information presented in this book will encourage owners and managers to use the tools and technology available to avoid having to take legal action from selecting a high-risk rental applicant.

Note: There is never a substitute for good legal advice. There are laws specific to renting out apartments that differ from state to state. If you own or manage real estate, you should have and use legal counsel to protect your own or your client's rights and assets. Do not be penny wise and pound foolish when protecting your investment. I have made efforts to highlight those areas where research in your state should be done. You should work with your attorney when you have specific questions regarding the renting process in your city and state *before* you take any action you think is questionable.

Carolyn Gibson
Author

Chapter 1

Why Homeowners Get the Wrong Rental Applicant

W hen you buy a piece of rental property, whether you live in it or not, it is a huge financial investment. Why then, do owners end up with tenants who do not pay their rent, destroy the apartment, and cause owners to pay massive legal fees, loss of rent money, inflict extreme stress, then leave your building to move into another newly prepared unit? What can a homeowner do to prevent renting to an irresponsible or high-risk tenant?

One of the most important decisions a homeowner with vacant apartments will make is to choose a tenant who will pay the rent, respect the property and the other tenants, and obey the laws of the land and the rules of their lease. However, around the country, there are countless numbers of homeowners who are keeping their vacant apartments empty. The primary reason is the fear or past experience of renting to the 'wrong' tenant.

If you have rental property, you want to get the most income out of it, while keeping expenses low on your investment. You may not always have the funds or desire to use an outside real estate broker. Many owners like to rent their own apartments to control who will live either with them and their family in the same building, or in an investment apartment.

By reading this book, you will learn basic and effective methods of the tenant selection process used by professional property managers. You will learn from an experienced renter of apartments, which decisions and procedures work best, and which techniques will *not* get you the kind of tenant you need and desire.

I have three primary reasons why I think homeowners, landlords, and/or managers end up with poor choices of tenants. For the most part, there are three areas of omission:

1. Owners do not check or verify all of the applicant's information;

2. Owners accept the rental applicant's explanations and excuses instead of searching for the facts;

3. Owners do not ask the right questions or enough questions

Some homeowners allow a total stranger to occupy their real estate financial investment. They take the minimal amount of time and spend as little money possible to investigate a rental applicant. If the applicant is friendly, smiles a lot, is personable, and appears to be 'neat and clean', he or she can get the keys to an apartment with little else than a security deposit and the first month's rent. There are owners who will rent their apartments to their relatives and/or friends of their children or neighbors, without checking anything at all.

Rental applicants come to you for a roof over their head on a month-to-month paying basis for a pre-determined amount of time. There is a cost to having shelter provided to an individual or family. Those who do not pay for their shelter must be asked to leave the premises, so that a more responsible family may benefit from the housing.

There are costs associated with providing decent, safe, and sanitary housing. We check out a rental applicant's information in order to attempt to ensure that we will receive the rent every month, on time, and that the tenant will respect the condition of the apartment and building. The return in spending the time and money in checking out a rental applicant as thoroughly as possible will be the long-term stability of your property, and especially your finances from that property.

It is important to remember what we gain from using a practical approach to renting out a vacant apartment. Here is a short list of what you can avoid when you take the time to pick a good tenant for a vacant apartment:

Aggravation	Frustration
Bank Foreclosure	Feeling of Helplessness
Bankruptcy	Legal Expenses
Repair Expenses	Prolonged Vacancy
Confrontations	Irritation
Anger	Loss of Savings
Resentment	Fear
Desperation	Arguments
Stress	Headaches

When you take the 'lazy' approach to picking a tenant, when you cut corners, spend less or no money to verify application information, when you listen to excuses, or just do not pay enough attention to the answers, you can rent an apartment to your peril. Many owners realize too late they have allowed an applicant to slip through the process. Perhaps the unit has been vacant for a long time. Maybe the unit is not one of the most desirable in your portfolio, or is in a neighborhood that makes renting it out difficult.

Carolyn Gibson

Whatever the reason, the time and money spent checking out every piece of information on the rental application is rewarded with a low-risk tenant. It is certainly cheaper than the eviction process.

Chapter 2

Make Your Tenant & Selection Process Decisions First

You need to make some decisions as to what kind of tenant you want. Then, you need to set some ground rules for your search. You need to decide on the process you intend to use to get the best tenant from a pool of applicants. If you are using a management company, you need to have this discussion with the people who will rent your apartments. You need to do all of this *before* you begin the rental application process.

Everyone connected with getting an apartment rented must be on the same page of the playbook. Everyone must be committed to taking or allowing the time and spending the money to find a good tenant. If all you want to do is fill a vacant apartment as fast as possible, almost any process, or no process, will suffice. You can take a good look at the applicant, decide whether or not he or she looks acceptable to you, get three recent pay stubs, first and last month's rent, a security deposit, then give him or her the keys to your apartment. This is how many people fill their vacancies when they are in a hurry for cash. This process is like rolling dice – a big gamble at your expense.

You want to rent to the best candidate. You want a person or people who have enough income to afford to pay the rent on a regular basis, will have respect for your property, and who wants to make a long term commitment to live quietly and obey the rules and laws. To get this type of person or family, you will need to commit to taking the appropriate time and spending the money necessary to find that person.

Every time I overlooked a part of the process, and accepted a rental applicant without doing a total due diligence, that missing detail always came back and bit me. Fortunately, I am a fast learner, and I learned to heighten my eye-for-details skill. Happily, by reading this book, you will get the benefit of learning from my unfortunate experiences.

Over the years as a management agent, owner/clients of multi-family developments have wanted to see their apartments rented as quickly as possible. This is good business. Especially after the new construction of a building, it is important to fill it up with tenants fast. Applicants for new construction properties are processed at least three months in advance of the projected opening of a new building. If the property is a government subsidized or low income tax credit property, there are additional pieces of verifications and certifications required as part of the overall selection method. Getting this information would sometimes cause delays in approving applicants.

If a client asked me if it were possible to sidestep a portion of a tenant selection process, I had to stand firm. I would explain why sticking to the entire process was important. If a client pressed me to 'jump' the applicant waiting list, or accept applicants with partially verified information as a way to rush the process, I would ask him or her to put that request in writing. Then, if (or when) we had problems with the rental applicant who received the preferred treatment, or the subsidy agency, the client would know that it was his or her decision to rent the unit to that person at the beginning of the process. I am happy to say that, once a client received clear information about the selection process, government requirements and procedures, at no time in more than twenty-five years did a client instruct me in writing to sidestep a tenant selection plan.

Why do we need to commit to a process? It is because, as human beings with specific natures, we have inherent weaknesses when we work together. Without a process, we are left to our personal prejudices, lack of experience renting out apartments, intuition, and other decisions that may not be in our best interest. With a process, you have a road map that helps to keep you on track and assists in helping you to make informed, fact-based decisions. It also gives an applicant the rules of the road. It should not be ambivalent or a secret as to what criteria will help a candidate get selected for an apartment.

What does an applicant think of us when we violate our own renting process? Most think that you will do it again in another matter. You must be completely committed to a renting process before you are faced with family or colleague peer pressure, sometimes-conflicting information, hard decisions and choices.

Who Will Interact with The Applicants?

There should be *only one person* as the primary contact with the rental applicants. You may make decisions as husband and wife or co-owners while reviewing the rental applications. Still, one person should interact with the applicants. A primary contact is essential in order to avoid confusion and any divide-and-conquer strategies by the applicant during the process. The worse thing you can do is to have a selection process in which anyone or everyone connected with the vacancy can make his or her own decisions along the way.

Carolyn Gibson

Is Your House in Legal Order?

It is your responsibility as a homeowner to comply with the city, state, and federal laws. Before you embark on the journey of finding a good tenant, make sure you are a good landlord. Are you renting an illegal basement or attic apartment? Is the building and apartment fixed up to the state building code? Have you complied with all city and state ordinances regarding zoning, health and safety, vacancy inspections, etc.?

Make sure your house is in order before you search for a tenant. If you are not certain the basement apartment has been legally installed, go to the state zoning department and look up your records. Apply for a zoning variance if the unit is not recorded as a legal apartment.

If you are installing or renovating a front porch for the vacancy, make sure the contractor has taken out a building permit for the work. In some states, if you have a metal fire escape, it must be inspected and certified by the Fire Department every few years. Check to see what is mandatory for your state, make the repairs, and get the appropriate certificate.

If you have a rent-controlled apartment, make sure you have applied for and *received* a vacancy decontrol certificate before you put someone in the unit. Do not increase the rent illegally if you are not authorized to do so by the state.

If you are renting to children under six years of age, do you have lead paint certificates, and are they current? Are there smoke detectors in the appropriate rooms, with new batteries installed? You don't want to go through the time,

8

trouble, and money to find a good tenant, only to discover that you need a current lead paint de-leading certificate before you can move in a person, especially a Section 8 tenant.

You will probably be advised that some of this work is not really necessary. Some will tell you that the city services are so backed up, the inspectors may never get to check your building. My job is to tell you that if you ignore doing what the law mandates, you do so at your own peril. You may get away with not doing the right thing for years. But, one day, if you have to evict a tenant, and your building code compliance is in question, it may have a significant impact on your ability to evict, or even collect rent.

One day, when someone is hurt on your property due to lack of repairs, it will cost you more than liability insurance. Make sure your property is in full compliance before you look for a tenant. Send in the applications for whatever certificates and inspections required. Protect your investment at the same time you seek to profit from your investment.

What Kind of Tenant Do You Want?

Once you make the commitment to rent out your vacancy, you need to think about, then be clear and steadfast as to the kind of tenant you want to occupy your investment

Assuming that every applicant has a good income, good landlord references and good credit, what kind of person are you looking for?

 ➢ You want a person or family who will pay the rent on time each month;

9

➢ You want a person or people who will respect your building and apartment by maintaining it in a decent, clean, safe, and sanitary manner;

➢ You want a person or people who will respect the other tenants in the building; by living quietly;

➢ You want a tenant who will call you if there is a repair problem needed in the apartment, such as a water leak or a cabinet loose from the wall;

➢ You want a tenant or tenants who will call you when there is an emergency situation, either in their apartment or the building;

➢ You want a tenant or tenants who will conduct themselves in accordance with their lease and the law;

There are numerous factors that could impact your decision to pick one applicant or family over another. These selection factors are different from discrimination based on a prejudice against a certain type of applicant, which is against the law. Some circumstances you may want to consider are whether or not the tenant or family live in the same building as you and your family, or whether or not the tenant(s) will share the building with your elderly parent(s). You may prefer a person or family with a history of long-term tenancies, or for stability in employment, income, etc.

You should think about these factors **before** you begin your search. You need to be prepared for those who are very good at convincing others to do things their way. When applicants try to convince you to choose them over someone else, you will need to review your list. You do not want to be persuaded to choose someone against your better judgment over a person whom you originally said you wanted as a tenant.

Here are some examples of types of rental applicants that may approach you. You should decide in advance how or if you will choose to process these specific applications.

Co-Signers

An applicant may ask if you accept co-signers. A co-signer is a person who will not live in the apartment, but guarantees that the rent will get paid if the applicant/tenant fails to do so. A co-signer is also guaranteeing that if there are any damages or unpaid rent above and beyond the amount of the security deposit, the co-signer will make those payments. A landlord does not have to agree to a co-signer. Whichever decision you make, to accept or not accept a co-signer, the policy should be made part of your selection plan.

This is a big financial *and* legal responsibility, usually accepted by a parent or parents for a child just out of college. The parent wants the young person to have his or her own apartment, and understands that he or she may not have a sufficient employment or credit history at the time. By signing a co-signer agreement, the parent agrees to put his/her own credit and finances on the line for the child.

A co-signer adds an additional party to your lease. If the applicant is accepted as your tenant, both the co-signer and the applicant will have to sign a lease addendum. You and the applicant agree to accept the co-signer as part of the lease, and the co-signer agrees to be responsible for the tenant's unpaid bills.

Your burden if something goes wrong is to pursue both the tenant and the co-signer if you are owed money. In some states, if the tenant files for bankruptcy, the co-signer can still be liable for the unpaid rent and/or damages.

If an applicant has no credit history because of his or her age, a co-signer would be in order. Neither you nor the applicant knows how rent will be handled. The co-signer would then be a good back-up person. But, if the applicant has a poor credit history, you already know he/she is an irresponsible person where bills are concerned. Rather than agree to a co-signer, let someone else assume the risk.

- ✓ The co-signer must be in compliance with your tenant selection policies: have good income, good credit, and employment. Why have a co-signer who is in the same or worse financial shape as your applicant?

- ✓ The co-signer should reside in the same state as your home. If you have to pursue the co-signer for your unpaid rent, you do not want to have to cross state lines to get your money;

- ✓ A co-signer should be responsible for the entire term of the lease;

- ✓ A co-signer should ideally be a family member, someone who cares what happens to the applicant and would pay to prevent the tenant from the non-payment of rent eviction process;

- ✓ Consider a co-signer for a roommate who is financially weak, thereby allowing both roommates to be eligible for the apartment, all other applicant information considered;

✓ A co-signer is only a financial back-up person. He/she does not have any rights to the apartment, such as keys, name on the mailbox, etc.;

The co-signer should only pay the rent if the tenant does not. You need to make it clear that the applicant is responsible for the monthly rent, and should make all rent payments. Check your state laws or your attorney on what would happen if the co-signer makes every rent payment. You do not want to establish a new tenancy by accepting regular co-signer payments.

Friends and Relatives

You need to be very clear that you establish a second, separate relationship when you rent to a friend or relative. Symbolically speaking, that person will cease to be your friend or relative, and will become your tenant. Decide in advance that you are willing to (perhaps) sacrifice the relationship for rent money before you move forward in this area.

➢ You sacrifice your privacy when you rent to a friend or relative in the same building where you live. They will know what you are doing, and you will know what they are doing on a regular basis;

➢ You allow the friend or relative into your financial business when they pay you rent;

➢ You allow the friend or relative to question your financial business when you apply a rent increase;

> The friend or relative allows you into their personal business and private life when he or she rents from you;

> Some landlords think that a "real" friend or relative shouldn't make so many maintenance complaints, or should fix things themselves. The friend or brother may think you should do it, because he is paying you rent every month;

> If the tenancy goes wrong, you could lose a friend, harm family relationships, and suffer financial, emotional and psychological hardships for a while, if not forever;

> The most heart wrenching housing court appearances I have witnessed have been between friends and relatives going through an eviction. Every issue (rent, noise, pets, etc.) is personal to both parties;

> Just because the person is related to you or has had the friendship of a decade will not necessarily mean he or she will be a good tenant;

> Every time your friend or relative has to fill out a check or money order for the rent, it is a reminder that you are their landlord. When or if something were to go wrong in the apartment, the friend will behave as if he or she should be given better, if not preferential treatment, because of his or her special status with you.

In general, be prepared for the thought process from your friend or relative that he or she should have a free pass to your rules. That could include being consistently late with the rent, asking you to put or allow special attachments in the apartment that no one else is allowed to do, disrespecting the other residents with loud music, and/or thinking you 'should have known' she likes to play her music loud while she is getting dressed in the morning.

Don't ever be deluded that your tenant is or will be a success because he or she is a friend or relative. The only reason it will work is if the person or family member would have been a good tenant anywhere they lived. If anything goes wrong with the apartment, or if the rent fails to be paid, rest assured you will behave like a landlord, and your friend or relative will behave like a tenant. You need to follow that scenario from the beginning to the end in your mind.

Write down all the things that could go wrong during their tenancy. What if they lose their job and can't pay the rent anymore, or your friend's son or daughter start to have a lot of their teenage friends hanging around the building? Think about what you know about your friend or relative and how that person may respond to your asking that person to pay the rent, or to better control their children and friends, or to pay for damages made in the apartment.

What will happen between you and your family if you have to evict your cousin, sister, brother, etc. for non-payment of rent? One relationship (business) crashes into your other relationship (family), and neither will come out right. I don't know of many win-win scenarios where an aunt can evict her niece with a child, and the family won't take sides. You have issues of family pressures, emotions, money, your real estate investment and mortgage payments, jealousy, ungratefulness, arguments, and anything else you can think of mixed into the equation.

What will make you angry more–the fact that your best friend won't obey the house rules, or pay the rent, or the fact that you rented the apartment in good faith, and now feel horribly betrayed? Which burden do you consider less – getting the rent paid on time and having the rest of your family think you are a mean, money grabbing scrooge, or find the friend or relative another place to live that you do not own?

If you can live with or think you can handle the landlord/friend or landlord/family relationship and still keep the relationships and your sanity, go ahead and process the application. If handling more than one major relationship at a time is not something you want to do, tell your friend or relative that you value him or her as a friend or relative, and for that reason do not want to get into a business relationship with him or her. Help the individual find another apartment somewhere else.

My opinion is that renting to friends or relatives is a mistake. This policy has worked for me for decades. I have only rented to one friend of a friend and one relative in over 25 years, and I have never regretted the decision. Both tenancies were a success. Why? Because I used a tenant selection process, and knew that these two people were good, mature tenants on their own merits.

Roommates and Live-In Lovers

Let us discuss renting to roommates and/or live-in lovers. Roommates and live-in lovers are two or more people who intend to legally share an apartment. There are very successful roommate situations that can and do last for years in one apartment. There are others that will not survive a month. What you have to discern is, into which category will your roommate or live-in lovers fall?

If two or more single people apply for the apartment, have each one complete their own rental application. Require that each person pass your eligibility criteria and selection process. This can become a sticky situation if one is not careful. What if you like one roommate, but are uncomfortable with the other? What if one roommate has impeccable credit and references, the other roommate is essentially indigent, and the eligible roommate intends to 'carry' his or her less successful roommate or lover?

Each and all of the roommates and live-in lovers for an apartment will sign one lease. The lease should clearly state that if one person moves out or is 'kicked out' by the other roommate(s), the remaining roommates are still responsible for the full rent amount and other aspects of the lease. The lease should also indicate whether or not they are allowed to replace a roommate before the end of the lease term, and under what conditions.

Roommates

Not everyone can afford to rent his or her own apartment. Roommates usually come together to save on or to share rent money. They do not always come together because they know each other. You need to ascertain if your roommate applicants have a history of rooming together, or if this is the first time they will share an apartment. Does either have any experience being a roommate, either at college, or at another apartment? Have they been roommates together at another apartment before this one? How long have they known each other?

Roommates should have a good idea of how they plan to run the apartment together. If they haven't discussed even the basics of living together, they will try to do it while they

17

are in the apartment, sometimes at your expense. For example, do they know how they intend to share the apartment expenses? Which one will interact with the landlord regarding the apartment?

You need to ask these questions and more during the Interview Process to see if they have a sense of what it means to be roommates. Do they appear to be compatible with each other when they discuss the apartment? Does one dominate the discussion over the other? Do they have a plan to cover the rent if one roommate loses a job? Would a financially weak applicant be willing to have a co-signer to the lease?

Co-ed roommates come with their own set of issues. If a man and a woman intend to share a two-bedroom apartment, this is fine. The trouble comes if a boyfriend or girlfriend enters the picture, and does not appear to like the arrangement. This is not your business. However, during the interview, you need to be clear that you are renting the apartment to the two of them, and not their love interests. Additions to the apartment would have to go through your selection process. This will make each applicant think twice about casually moving in people without your knowledge or permission. It will also make their roommate situation more serious to them.

You should make it very clear that if a roommate moves out, you still maintain final approval of the new roommate *before* he or she can move in. Require that the proposed new roommate complete a rental application and be processed before you give your move-in approval. This information should be added to your lease agreement as an addendum, or it will be considered a verbal agreement that will be forgotten a year or even six months later.

Again, there are many successful roommate situations, especially in college cities with sparse dormitory space like Boston, Washington, DC, New York, and others with large universities in the center of town. Colleges will allow students to room together outside of the college campus due to overcrowded conditions on campus. If the roommates were once dormitory students before they decided to get an apartment, the college can give a landlord reference. The question that has to be answered is still the same: will the roommates make good tenants?

See the section on co-signers in this chapter. If you have one applicant with a steady income, and the other roommate is financially shaky, but otherwise a good applicant, perhaps a co-signer for that roommate is in order.

Live-In Lovers

Let's discuss the live-in lover situation. Is a live-in lover different than a roommate? Not really. Two people still share the apartment, both and each are still responsible for the apartment expenses, and both will be covered under your lease. The only difference I see is that the two tenants sleep in the same bed and "play house" together.

Again, you want to know some details. Will this be their first apartment together? How long have they been living together? What will happen if they breakup? Can either one support the apartment alone if they break up? You want to make it clear that you are accepting their application as a couple as well as individuals. Both and each will be responsible for the apartment.

In a similar situation, I have seen some owners go absolutely bonkers, when the tenant's boyfriend or girlfriend starts to stay or bring furniture into the unit. This is a situation that happens after the lease is signed that the applicant will live as a single person. Owners sometimes base the amount of rent on how many people will occupy the apartment. Additional people to the unit means increases in the water bill, wear and tear, etc. Besides, the applicant indicated he or she would live alone. Now, after a few months, he or she has moved in someone else without your permission.

It is better to discuss this possibility up front, rather than to act coy about it and pretend it may not happen. Especially if the boyfriend or girlfriend shows up with the applicant to see the apartment, you should ask if they plan to rent it together. This is not the time to be shy, or to avoid a possible future situation. Certainly, one has brought the other for their approval. Let's not pretend he or she won't be there if the applicant gets the unit.

Some owners charge a new rent if the lover decides at a later date to move-in. There is an extra cost associated with an extra person living in the apartment. Extra use of the utilities, extra wear and tear on the apartment are two examples. Let the applicant know up front that if he or she is selected as a single person, the rent will be "x"; if the lover moves in later on, the rent will be "y", *and* he or she will have to be processed, *and* a new lease signed with a new security deposit. You want to control who is staying in your apartment under your conditions.

This would be the same if the applicant brings his or her mother, sister, etc. to stay permanently. You have the right to limit your apartment to two people per bedroom. Obviously, if the visit is short-term, you will not have to go through the trouble and expense of taking an application and verifying the information.

The Tenant Who Cleans and Does Repairs

One of the decisions you might consider before you bring on a new tenant is to have the person clean the building and take out the trash in exchange for not paying a portion or all of the rent. You may decide that you want a person or family with an able-bodied man or woman to do this work. Perhaps the applicant is only looking for an apartment where he or she can deduct a portion or all of the rent in exchange for being the building handy person. Let's look at the possibilities of this thought pattern.

There are owners who look for this kind of arrangement, thinking it can and will save them hard labor or aggravation at the property. They figure that if they can find a person who needs a break on the rent, they might be willing to put in some 'sweat equity' for a lower rent. You then as the owner, will have less on-site duties and responsibilities. Likewise for the owner that decides he or she wants a handy man type person to repair the vacancy before it is occupied.

There are a number of legal, financial, and technical problems with this choice of a tenant. First of all, if he or she is working at the property, what is he/she - a site manager, or a resident superintendent in addition to being a tenant? Is this person your tenant or your employee? If so, then what does that make you - the owner, the employer, or both?

If something doesn't work out, or work is not done at all or to your satisfaction, you are the supervisor of your tenant. If you decide it isn't working out, where do you go with the tenant-to housing court or the unemployment office?

21

There are issues of liability when a tenant does work at the property. What happens if he or she slips and falls on the stairs while cleaning them? Or falls off a ladder and hurts his back while changing a light bulb? Chances are, you could be looking at a long-time or permanent back injury. Does your building or homeowners' insurance cover this kind of injury? Should you carry workers compensation insurance on the tenant in addition to homeowners' insurance to cover this kind of liability (Yes!)? If you decide to go ahead and get this insurance, will the extra cost plus the loss of rent make doing this financially viable?

Some other questions for you to consider are:

* What if you discover that, after the property is brought up to par, there is not enough work to be done at the property to justify the amount of rent that is deducted each month?

* Who cleans and repairs the building if the tenant gets sick or when he or she goes on vacation?

* What if the tenant decides not to shovel snow that has been falling all day until after he/she comes home from work? Your sidewalk has been covered with snow all day and a good part of the evening. What if the tenant has to work overtime? What if, after cutting the grass, it is not picked up, it rains, and someone slips and falls on it?

* What will you do if the other tenants complain about their cleaning and repair neighbor?

* How will your other tenants feel about allowing their neighbor into their apartment to do work?

* Who buys his/her supplies? How much can he or she spend on his/her own?

* If your tenant overspends on your behalf, how will he/she get reimbursed?

* What will you do if the tenant loses or does not turn in his receipts for purchases made for the property?

* Who checks on your tenant's work? How will you know work is getting done the way you want?

* What if your tenant has someone else, like his teenaged son, do the work?

I do not recommend paying your tenant "under the table" for this work. This means, giving the tenant cash for work done at the property. Most people, when they say they are being paid "under the table", mean they receive undeclared income, and the employer isn't paying taxes on behalf of the employee. This is different from working as an independent contractor. In that case, the tenant receives cash, and has to declare his annual income to the IRS on a 1099 income tax form provided by the employer.

If you pay money or forgive all or a portion of the rent, you will also have to declare the rent he does not have to pay as his income, and you get to deduct the rent not paid to you as a tax deduction. You will have to issue the tenant an IRS 1099 form for each year of service.

If you want to go this way, contact the IRS and find out what they say about independent contractors. Will the tenant have to carry his own insurance? When you buy a house with tenants, you have to itemize your expenses. This makes your real estate investment a small business. If the IRS decides to review your income tax records, you must have your receipts and records in order. Having a tenant who also works at the property will add to your record keeping and potential liability responsibilities.

For more information, read Chapter 12, the first section titled *"Avoid Side Deals"*. If after reading this section you are still determined to use a tenant to do work at your property, you need to consult with your attorney to make sure you comply with your state laws.

Tenant With a Home Business

Today, there are more than 24 million home based businesses operating in the United States[1]. At some point, an applicant with a home-based business will apply for your vacant apartment. You will want and need to know the nature and extent of your potential tenant's home business. You will need to know what kind of business it is, if there will be outside visitors to the apartment, and whether or not it is a legal enterprise.

You have to be mindful of the type of building you are renting out, the kind of tenants who already live in the building, where your building is located, what floor the new tenant will occupy, the amount of space or bedrooms you are renting, etc. Is the neighborhood zoned for the applicant's home based business? Does the neighborhood have mixed use zoning, which is legal use for both residential and commercial activities?

---

[1] American Association of Home Based Businesses

Positives of a Home-Based Business

You should not reject a home-based business out of hand without looking into it and asking questions about how the tenant plans to run the business. The home-based business is here to stay, and is growing every year. Invariably, you will be faced with an applicant whose sole source of income is a business worked out of the apartment.

In fact, home-based businesses could be one of your most stable types of tenancy. The average home-based business owner has ten years of experience in their chosen profession. A person with a home-based business will not want to move in the near future. There are some businesses that depend on being able to stay in one place for a number of years. There are some home-based businesses such as bookkeeping or financial consulting, where the clients want to see stability in their independent contractor's living arrangements.

Thousands of home-based businesses do not interact with clients at their home. Their home is merely where their office is located, where they do their business work, maintain files, prepare proposals, etc. Many consultants and independent contractors visit or work at their client's place of business. There are businesses that are strictly Internet based, with very little contact with 'the outside world'.

If you are renting a single-family house, or the first floor of a two family house, there may be room for a home-based business. An applicant will be attracted to a first floor unit for the easy access for their customers.

A tenant with a home based-business will be careful to take good care of the apartment, because there will be visitors. The kind of home they present to their clients must be in good shape to show they have a prosperous business. Also, you can require that the tenant add a security system to their unit to prevent liability claims against the ownership. Most home-based businesses will not mind adding this to their apartment, or even one or two ABC fire extinguishers at their own expense.

You may be able to negotiate a higher rent from a home-based business to cover the extra expenses of increased utility use, and maintaining the unit and building. An entrepreneur may not mind paying the extra rent in exchange for being able to run their business from home. He or she can allocate a portion of the rent toward business use on his/her income taxes as a business expense.

Negatives of a Home-Based Business

If you or your tenants work nights, and the incoming tenant gives piano lessons during the day or runs a day care center for babies from her home, there could be a conflict. Everyone in the building must be considered.

Depending upon who pays the utility bills, understand that running a home business tends to increase utility expenses. This is because the tenant is essentially home all day. When it's cold outside, the heat will be on 24 hours a day. The computer will run constantly, increasing the electric bill. If you have a property with one utility bill for the entire building, you will need to install separate meters for each apartment. You may be able to have the applicant agree to pay for a portion of this work if he or she wishes to sign a long-term lease[2].

---

[2] Consult your attorney for state regulations on meter sharing between a residency and a business

You will have extra wear and tear on the apartment and the property itself, depending on the type of home business. Extra traffic in and out of the building is one thing that will wear out a floor, stairs, etc. You will only be able to charge a certain amount of security deposit according to your state law. Most laws allow only one month's rent as a security deposit.

Questions to Ask: How old is the business? Is it just starting out? Is the nature of the business one in which inventory is kept? Where will the items be stored? Will the tenant keep boxes of paper goods in the apartment? Are there specific hazardous waste materials involved in the business? How will they be disposed?

What will happen if the home based business is the tenant's sole source of income, and the firm or tenant or both declares bankruptcy? Is the business one that is recession proof, or has been in existence for enough years to have a loyal clientele? Read Chapter 8, the section on 'Bankruptcy'. Talk to your lawyer about what your rights would be in your state under the bankruptcy laws.

What You Need to Know and Have to Make a Decision

As a home-based business owner myself, I see the positives as well as the negatives from my perspective as a homeowner and a business owner. Get as much information needed to give you the comfort level to consider this type of applicant.

You want proof that the applicant has a 'real' business. A copy of the company's Article of Organization, incorporation documentation, or similar legal document signed and sealed by the state must be provided.

Does the applicant have a home-based business now? If yes, have the applicant prove that he or she carries liability insurance for the current apartment and building. You do not want the tenant carried on your homeowners' policy. If one of their customers slips and falls, you want your business tenant to be sued. At the very least, you will want your tenant to indemnify, or cover you under their liability policy for such events. Talk to your insurance agent about insurance indemnification coverage if you rent to a home-based business.

If the business is incorporated, most states require that the principal carry workers compensation insurance for him or herself as well as employees. Other questions or proof of business may include:

> ➤ Will the tenant have a lot of cash at the home as part of the business?

> ➤ Will they need to make any modifications for their business, such as extra electrical or telephone outlets, special lighting, etc.?

> ➤ What are the zoning laws for your neighborhood?

> ➤ Does the applicant have income tax records as proof of self-employment?

> ➤ Have the tenant use a post office box for mail to prevent a backlog of bulk, priority, or express mail coming to the building.

> ➤ Will having no outside business visitors either before or after a specific time of day or night hinder their business?

Applicants with Disabilities

You may have handicapped or disabled applicants who wish to rent your second or third floor apartment. If/when they attend your Open House, you must not differentiate your treatment of such applicants from anyone else.

Handicap status

The following section is taken from the Department of Housing & Urban Development, Section 8 Handbook 4350.3 CHG-24, Section 2-44, 1/93. It addresses the federal laws regarding treatment of handicap rental applicants with disabilities.

Except as indicated in paragraph 2-25f, it is unlawful to make an inquiry to determine whether an applicant for a dwelling unit, a person intending to reside in that dwelling unit after it is rented or made available, or any persons associated with that person, has a handicap or to make inquiry as to the nature or severity of a handicap of such a person.

It shall be unlawful for an owner/manager to refuse to make reasonable accommodations in rules, policies, practices, or services, when such accommodations may be necessary to afford an individual with handicaps equal opportunity to use and enjoy a dwelling unit, including public and common use areas. (Fair Housing Act.)

Carolyn Gibson

Applicants with Assistive Animals

The following section is taken from the Department of Housing & Urban Development, Section 8 Handbook 4350.3 CHG-24, Section 2-43, 1/93. It addresses the federal laws regarding the acceptance of assistive animals for rental applicants with disabilities.

1) Some individuals with handicaps may use an assistive animal (e.g., guide dogs for persons with vision impairments, hearing dogs for persons with hearing impairments, and emotional support animals for persons with chronic mental illness).

2) Owners may require individuals with handicaps.. in family housing to provide justification that the animal may be needed for the individual to have equal opportunity to use and enjoy the housing (e.g., letter from medical provider). If owners make these inquiries, they must apply them uniformly to all persons with assistive animals.

Section 8 Applicants, Certificates and Vouchers

The Section 8 program is a federal government subsidy program that helps low-income persons to better afford to rent an apartment competitively in the general market. It allows an applicant to seek housing in areas and properties outside of the public housing and government subsidized housing system.

The term "very low-income' is used to describe the maximum amount of income a person must earn in order to be determined eligible for a Section 8 certificate. The income level is different for each county and state in the

United States. Very low-income families have incomes below 50% of the city area median income[3]. The income level is based on the median, or average, income in that specific county or city, is set by HUD, and changes yearly.

A certificate is issued to a qualified low-income applicant with a specific approved maximum rent. It is the responsibility of the applicant to shop around for an apartment with a rent within that issued on the Section 8 certificate. A Section 8 certificate holder has 60 days to find an apartment and use the certificate. Extensions of time are granted sparingly.

Similar to the Section 8 certificate program, the U.S. Department of Housing and Urban Development (HUD) also offers a tenant owned voucher as well as a certificate. With a voucher, the holder is allowed to pay more than the maximum contracted rent listed on the voucher. The extra rent would have to be included in the lease as a tenant share. HUD will not pay more than what it has agreed to on its voucher document.

Whether a certificate or a voucher, the tenant pays 30% of his or her income towards the rent. The Section 8 certificate or voucher agency will pay 70%, the rest of the total apartment rent. If you accept a Section 8 certificate or voucher, this means that you will have a third party as a tenant. You will receive a rent check from the tenant, and one from the Section 8 agency each month.

The government agency portion of the rent is contingent upon the apartment being maintained in accordance with the state sanitary or health codes of your state. You and the Section 8 agency will sign a Housing Assistance Payment

---

[3] http://www.hud.gov/offices/pih/programs/hcv/tenant.cfm

(HAP) Contract. This contract enables you to charge and receive the other 70% of your total rent. You will actually have two tenants – the person living in your apartment, and the federal government.

Your building and the apartment must be inspected before the Section 8 tenant can move in. Your building and the apartment will be inspected each year for a examination of any violation of the building codes. If an inspector finds something wrong in the apartment, such as the presence of vermin, a broken washer in a sink, or a missing spoke in the hallway handrail, you will be given notice and a specific amount of time to correct the problem. When that time expires, and the work has yet to be completed or has not been started, the government agency will hold back their portion of the rent until the unit and/or building is back in building code compliance. In many instances, once a "stop payment" is issued, you will not get your rent back retroactive to the date the payment was stopped. It will begin the day the inspection is considered passed.

You should still have a Section 8 certificate or voucher holder complete your rental application. You are still responsible for screening a Section 8 applicant as you would any of your other applicants.

Sample Tenant Selection Criteria

Here is one example of how a Tenant Selection Criteria[4] would look for a two bedroom. It can be as simple or as complicated as you want:

---

[4] This Sample is For Discussion Purposes Only.

Owner Contact Person (Choose Only One):

o   ☐ Husband ☐ Wife ☐ Sister ☐ Manager ☐ Broker

o   Final decision as to which tenant is selected will be made by:

     ☐ The Manager ☐ The Owner ☐ Husband & Wife

Required:

- o Every person interested in renting the apartment must complete a rental application;

- o If roommates, each roommate must complete his or her own rental application;

- o Applicant must have been employed at same company for at least three years, or show a stable source of income, such as a pension;

- o Applicant must have had his or her own apartment at some point in time;

- o Applicant must show proof that he or she has the first month's rent and security deposit in hand before the process begins. This can be proved by a letter from the bank, or a copy of the current bank statement;

- o If a Section 8 certificate or voucher applicant, a copy of the document must be submitted;

- o The entire application must be verified by third parties;

o Every applicant will have a source of income verification, credit report, eviction report, criminal background check, and landlord reports completed;

o Home visits are <u>not</u> required.

Eligibility:

o ☐ Will ☐ Will not accept co-signers for the apartment. Each applicant must stand on his or her own merits;

o Applicant(s) must have a minimum combined income of between $40,000 and $65,000 per year, unless using a Section 8 certificate or voucher;

o A home based business is okay, if it will not interfere with the quiet enjoyment of the other tenants, use excessive utilities, nor bring excessive foot traffic or wear and tear to the property;

o No home based business that needs water in order to run the business from the apartment, or needs to solicit the public for business;

o Applicant must have a good credit report, not necessarily flawless;

o A single applicant can rent a three bedroom apartment if finances support it;

o Real estate brokers ☐ Will ☐ Will not be considered to assist with the renting process

Non-Negotiable:

- o Friends and/or relatives must go through the same selection process as everyone else;

- o No applicant who wants to do work on the property in exchange for a lower rent;

- o There will be a Family Interview for the top three applicants;

- o Only a maximum of two persons per bedroom are allowed. Owner will not determine who must sleep in which bedroom;

- o Will only rent to the bedroom size on the Section 8 certificate or voucher.

Now you are ready to start looking for your next tenant!

Carolyn Gibson

CHAPTER 3

When and Where to Advertise for Applicants

You should start to look for a tenant as soon as your current tenant gives you thirty days notice. That way, you can begin the application process with the goal of fixing up the vacancy in one month, and finding a new tenant one month after the tenant moves out. That gives you sixty days advance opportunity to find a good tenant.

Always require your departing tenant to give you thirty days notice in writing. Once notice is committed to writing, everyone has a sense that it will really happen. If the tenant does not give you notice in writing, you should send a confirmation letter to the tenant. The letter should confirm that on such-and-such a date, the tenant informed you that he or she would be leaving the apartment on the 30th of the month. Any changes to that date should be put in writing, with a copy in the tenant's file folder.

Do not waste time looking for a new tenant. You want to get a good cross sample of candidates and contenders. You should cast a wide net, especially if finding applicants is difficult in your area. At the same time, realize that where you advertise will determine the kind of applicants you will get in response. If you are looking for Section 8 tenants, advertise at the local housing authorities. If you don't mind having college students, advertise at the local universities' housing department.

The location of the apartment, the amount of rent you charge, any amenities you include, your selection criteria and other factors will determine who will actually decide to apply for your apartment. The more information you give out in advance, the better applicants will pre-screen for you.

Agency Affiliation

One of my most successful affiliations with regard to filling vacancies was with an organization that had a program for women in shelters. They needed apartments to help these ladies transition into permanent placements. I rented three apartments in a small building to the program organization, and they supplied the tenants for each vacancy that came up over a period of years.

The agency was responsible for paying the rent and any damages to the apartment. On the whole, the young ladies selected for the apartments were responsible, quiet, eager to succeed, and cooperative. The program manager would remove any tenant who was not prepared to adhere to the lease. It was a perfect blend of keeping the vacancies rented, with a client who was totally responsible for the tenant, the rent, and the condition of the apartment. This is one method of finding good tenants for your units, by establishing a relationship with an agency that needs to place a few of their participants in vacancies in the same building over a period of years.

Newspapers

Your ad should be clear, and aimed toward getting applicants fast. Some newspaper ads have so little information, or are so full of jargon, that I am hard pressed to understand what is being rented. Spend the money to explain what you are trying to rent, so the person reading the ad can know what is being offered.

Classified ads are the best, regardless of the type of newspaper. They are placed under the city where the apartment is located, under the Apartments for Rent section, and are the most inexpensive. Community newspapers are the best types of newspapers to put a classified ad. Here are some examples of what I think are ads where too little money has been spent explaining what is being rented[5]:

Boston. 2br, no util., hwf, ac, eik, w/d
$1500   617-555-1234.
What are these initials?

Fenway. 3br, near trans, LR, DR, S8, no pets
$2100   617-555-4321
What kind of transportation is it near?

Quincy 2/3 bedroom from
$1100 to $1250   617-555-4592
Is this a two bedroom for $1100 and a three bedroom for $1250, or two or three bedrooms are available?

These ads will attract callers trying to find out what they mean. The owner can then make his or her sales pitch directly to the interested party. I prefer to provide as much information as possible to cut down on questions. Here are some good advertisements that provide enough information for an applicant to get a real sense of the apartment and what is offered with it. They also caught my eye with amenities of interest to me if I were looking for an apartment:

---

[5] Ads are newspaper advertisement composites

Carolyn Gibson

Boston 1br, lr/dr, kit, ldry, hwflrs, pkg, 1 block to beach. Nr T station. No fee. $1300 617-555-2233

Waltham Ultra modern 1 bedroom, w/fully applianced kit. Lots of charm! No Pets. No Fee $995 508-555-2918

East Bridgewater Lrg & lovely grand 11 rm Col. Space for ofc, extended fam & easy access to Boston $4000/mo 222-555-1975

If you call enough ads, you will get a sense of what these anachronisms represent. Brokers and owners on the whole, are happy to explain their abbreviations to you. Here is a translation of the ads listed above:

Util = utilities
lr, dr = living room, dining room
rm = room
Ldry = laundry
pkg = parking
S8 = Section 8 applicants
Kit = kitchen
ofc = office
W/d = washer/dryer (usually in the apartment)

eik = eat-in kitchen
Br = bedroom
fam = family
hwflrs = hard wood floors
No fee = no application fee
ac = air conditioning
Col = Colonial type home

hkups = washer and dryer hook ups only

Fair Housing

If you advertise in a newspaper, regardless of its size, you need to be careful that you do not violate the federal Fair Housing laws. There are still many newspapers that are not up on the federal laws regarding how they can advertise for apartments. They are supposed to know, even if you do not. In any case, both parties could be held liable for an advertisement that is not in compliance with the federal or state laws.

It is illegal to advertise in a manner that discriminates against any person because of race, color, religion, sex, disability, handicap, familial status (composition of family), or national origin;

The newspaper should have a copy of its non-discrimination policy in their advertising section for rentals, or should provide a copy to you.

Weekend classified ads are the best because it has the largest circulation of papers. Also, there are other days that the paper can tell you are the second highest circulation. These days may be less expensive than a weekend ad. The paper will work with you to put together a special or discount rate based upon the length of your ad, number of times you run it, which days it is run, etc. Talk to the classified ad person and let them help you place an effective ad within your budget. Usually you get immediate responses the day or day after the ad comes out.

Sign in the Window

A familiar sight in every city is the 'For Rent' sign in the window of the property that is vacant. I used to do this myself, as it always brought a lot of interested parties to me. At the same time, I realized that it brought a number of other things for me to handle.

- People will ring the doorbells of the building, trying to get someone to show them the apartment, or for more information. This is an annoyance to your current residents;

- It brings extra traffic to the property, not all of it good traffic or legitimate interest;

41

- Applicants will come by at all times of the day and night to make inquiries, usually when you are watching your favorite television program, or while having dinner with your family;

- You have no control as to who will respond to your ad. You get whomever drives by at the time;

- Regardless of the location of the property, there is always the criminal element that figures out you have an empty apartment. It is an open invitation for them to break in and enter your building, vandalize the unit, steal your copper pipes, or appliances.

The good news is that you will get interested applicants, eager enough to stop what they are doing to make inquiries. Having seen the building and the apartment in question, they are already attracted to the unit. Many people depend on the "For Rent" sign in the window or on a door if they want to live in a specific neighborhood. They look for a place near their job, school, day care facilities, etc. and will drive around to see what is available.

A good number of owners, managers, and management companies advertise with a sign in the window, with a contact telephone number. It works, and it's an inexpensive way to get applicants.

Bulletin Boards and Flyers

Flyers on bulletin boards are excellent advertising. You can do so for the cost of copying the flyers. You can put your flyer up on just about any community bulletin board. Make sure you bring your own thumbtacks or push pins to hang up your flyer. Some locations have several bulletin boards to place flyers. Some places you will have to ask permission to hang a flyer. Others will want an expiration date on it.

Here are some good bulletin board locations where you can present your apartment to a large number of people, and a cross section of diverse rental applicants:

Good Bulletin Board Locations

Church	Hospitals
Veterans Hospitals	Supermarkets
Graduate Schools	Post Office
Housing Authorities	Police Stations
YMCA/YWCA	Local Gym
Military Recruitment Office	Beauty Salons
Pharmacies	Restaurants
Multi-Service Agencies	Barber Shops
Colleges/Universities	Deli Shop
Management Companies	Welfare Office
Health Care Centers	Variety Stores
Day Care Centers	Shopping Malls
Senior Citizen Agencies	Laundromats
Where You Work	24 Hour Stores

Exhibit 1 at the back of the book is an example of a flyer that I wouldn't use for the Public. There are so many rules and restrictions that an applicant would be afraid or very reluctant to look any further for an apartment from this person. It is a case of Too Much Information Too Soon. This flyer I would have at the vacant unit on the wall. You don't want to chase people away before they even get to see how wonderful an apartment you have available.

43

Word of Mouth and Referrals

This is still a powerful way to find good rental applicants. Those who know you are still the best people to recommend a tenant to you. They know your standards and your expectations of a tenant. Your friends and relatives will try to refer a person who will be successful renting from you. Friends are always happy to help their friends in need.

You can spread the word about your apartment yourself. Everyone knows a host of people you can tell about your vacant apartment. It can come up in casual conversation with your doctor, attorney, dentist, at the beauty salon, your job, where you do volunteer work, etc. You are probably the best form of advertising by letting people know you have an opening.

Your other tenants are good word of mouth referrals. Your tenants will want someone who is compatible with them. When you put your "For Rent" sign in the window, they will let their friends, relatives, and co-workers know there is a vacancy in their building. A referral is not the same as a personal reference. The applicant, regardless of who made the referral, still has to qualify according to your selection process and standards.

There are owners who pay a referral fee to a tenant who has successfully found a tenant for you. Success is determined when the referred person moves into the apartment. A nominal $50 fee is usually given.

Other Ways to Advertise Your Vacancy

Your local legislative person, State Representative, City Counselor, Alderman, or State Senator are more than happy to get information on a vacant apartment. Many times, they are looking for a place for one of their constituents. If you make it a habit of sending him or her a flyer each time you have a vacant apartment, he or she will send you potential applicants from your district. Make sure you are clear about the income level you need the applicant to make to be eligible for your apartment.

If you have a web site, use it to advertise your vacancy to those who frequent your site and are familiar with you.

How Many Applications Do You Need?

Industry standards indicate that an owner or property manager should process at least three rental applications for each vacant apartment to fill. You will want to do a thorough background check on your top three applicants. You should have at least six to nine rental applications available from which to pick your top three people to fill one apartment.

How many rental applications will you need to have available for people to fill out? You will get a feel for this based upon the responses to your advertising. The most important thing is not to run out of applications while people are still showing up and interested in your vacancy. If you have received at least a dozen telephone calls for your apartment, I would have at least twenty rental applications on hand. For every person who calls, he or she might bring a friend or relative who is also looking for an apartment.

Screen Applicants By Telephone

I put a small advertisement in the city Sunday newspaper. The next day when I got home from work, I had over 50 calls on my machine! Calls were coming in even as I was answering them, especially from the people who had already left a message. Everyone wanted to make sure he or she had first crack at renting the three-bedroom apartment. It was madness.

I knew if this were to continue for a week, I would never get back to all the callers. I decided to leave a message on my answering machine that I would hold an open house at the property on a specific day and time. When I called back to the ones who had already left a message, I let them know their questions would be answered on the open house day.

This is what happens in a city or community where apartments are scarce. If you live in a city where there are plenty of vacant apartments, one small advertisement in a community newspaper may not be noticed among all of the other advertisements for vacant apartments. You may have to advertise in more than one newspaper, or place an ad with more details about the apartment.

If you have teenagers, you can appreciate the fact that they love to talk on the telephone. So much so, that if they are talking on the phone, and another call comes in for you, there is no guarantee you will ever get the message. That is if you have Call Waiting. If not, you will not even know whether or not anyone has called, because all they will get is a busy signal. With Call Waiting, *maybe* you will get the message a few days after your child received it!

To avoid missing important calls when I am renting an apartment, I bought a multiple caller answering machine. You can also sign up for a multiple caller voice mail service through your phone company. Both do the same thing. Each allows a caller to hear a specific message regarding the vacancy, and to leave a message to the person renting out the unit. You can tell callers which button to push to leave a message about the vacancy, including their name, telephone number, and the best time for you to call back.

When you talk to applicants over the telephone, remember this is your time to give your sales pitch. You want to make the apartment attractive to eligible applicants, so the people you speak with will want to see the apartment. This is your best marketing approach, and your chance to make a good first impression on your potential applicants.

This is your time to get as much information about the applicant possible. You want to ascertain eligibility, and see if the fit is good for both parties. Answer their questions as you seek to get answers. Be pleasant, enthusiastic, and eager to meet the applicant.

Give Out a Key

Would you take $25 and give a total stranger the keys to your car to try it out? Why then, would you take a $25 key deposit, and then give an applicant the keys to your vacant apartment and building to look at it without you? You don't know when or if an applicant will make a copy of the key while out to look at the unit, even if you intend to change the unit door lock once it is rented. The person(s) will still have the entry door key at their disposal. For a $25 or even $50 deposit, some applicants will still forget to return your key to you until a few days later. Always maintain control over your vacant apartment.

Similarly, I do not advise that you give a key to your vacancy to another tenant in the building for them to show the apartment. I do not think this is a good policy, as it goes back to maintaining control over your own property. When you ask a tenant to show your apartment, you are giving that person authorization to represent you as the owner. This person will also have access to the applicant's personal information. This is dangerous. A good relationship today with a tenant could go sour the next week. Do not leave yourself open to vulnerability, not to mention legal action, by making your tenant a partner in your investment.

Keep the vacant apartment locked when you are not showing it. Tell your tenant(s) to let you know if someone has been trying to gain entry to the vacant apartment when you are not there. Better, have them call the police, and then you.

Prepare Your Building for Company

Let's say the property is in a distressed community, or needs some work. The applicant drives by, sees the building, and decides that the appearance of the property is less than to be desired. You may have missed out on a good applicant who is basing the condition of the unit by the outside curb appeal. Yet, unknown to the potential applicant, you have renovated the apartment to the highest level. If only he or she had allowed you the chance to talk to him or her before looking at the building.

Curb Appeal is what the property looks like on the outside. With good curb appeal, an applicant will tend to think the rest of the property inside looks as good as the outside. With poor curb appeal, the rental applicant will think the rest of the property, including the vacant apartment, looks as bad as the outside.

This happened to my sister and me when we began the search for a house. The broker showed us a three-family building that hadn't been painted in years; the shrubbery obstructed the first floor windows, the doorbells were missing, and on and on. I balked at even getting out of my car to go inside. We had agreed we would look at "fix-ups", but this house looked more like a loser.

Fortunately for my sister and me, the broker insisted that we go inside and take a look. Inside were two beautiful apartments with large rooms, well-kept hard wood floors, new kitchen shelves, and other equally impressive attributes. My sister and I immediately fell in love with the property, and agreed that although the outside would need to be fixed up, the inside apartments were the real treasure.

The same premise happens with the renting of apartments. When you give out the address of your vacant apartment before it or the property is ready to be shown, if the outside is in disrepair, make sure you give a disclaimer or explanation of the building's condition. You want the applicant to get the full effect and impact of your vacant unit, not necessarily the building, at this time.

If you do not live in the building where the vacancy exists, you need to understand that every building has a day life and nightlife. Everything may be quiet and peaceful during the day. Yet, once the sun goes down, the building, or perhaps the entire street, may come alive. You may have tenants sitting on the front steps, drinking, playing loud music, with their children playing games at the top of their lungs until 11:00 pm. Your building may appear dark and gloomy because the outside lights need bulbs, or there are insufficient lights on.

Make sure you have a building ready to be shown to strangers. If that means asking tenants not to hang out on the front steps, if it means installing halogen lighting instead of floodlights, do the work. Raise the standards of your current and future tenants by keeping your property in good shape and demanding proper tenant behavior.

Chapter 4

Open House - Prepare for the Applicants

Y ou have to plan for visitors to your apartment. First, the building, inside and out, should be clean and presentable for viewing. Your apartment could be large and gorgeous, and with an affordable rent. But, if you do not have a building that looks good from the outside, some people will keep on driving away from it. If you cannot get the repairs done for the building, then the main thing to do is to make sure the apartment is presentable. In other words, ideally, it should be fixed up and ready for someone to move in when you show it.

The rental applicant should already know what he or she is going to rent. It is not fair to show an apartment "in progress", and expect him or her to have a good sense of what it will look like when it is finished. How many times has an owner said "I'll fix that before you move in", only to forget to do it? My experience has been that no matter what their personal circumstances, most people want to see what they will be paying for in advance. First impressions still count in renting apartments, even in a market where there are few vacancies.

Showing the apartment when it is completed is a good way to start off the relationship between the owner and rental applicant. It starts the possible association on a positive note, and is a good faith "show-and-tell" situation. The applicant does not have to guess or imagine what the unit will look like once it is finished.

On the other hand, who really has the luxury of waiting until an apartment is completely finished before marketing it to the public? Many small homeowners have to show it while it is in production, so that hopefully by the time it is complete, the owner will have someone ready to move right into it. Time is money, and the longer an apartment is vacant, the more money an owner will lose.

The least you can do is make sure the apartment is clean, and you don't have a lot of debris on the floor when you show it. Let the applicant know where you are in the completion process. Is the apartment you are showing almost finished? Did you just get started? This information will let the applicant see some of the quality of the work being done, and what you consider a finished product.

It is important to understand that there is a risk involved in showing an unfinished apartment. It could decrease the number of eligible applicants who will want to rent it out. The finished product should be in excellent condition. If you showed an applicant an unfinished vacancy, you will have to make doubly sure that you <u>and</u> the tenant complete an apartment inspection report[6] before anyone gets a key. This way, the memory of what was unfinished, dirty, in poor condition, etc. will be diminished by the facts in the apartment inspection report.

✓ Make sure you have enough rental applications, file folders and release forms available to be completed. If you have received a lot of calls before the Open House, you should have a good idea how many blank applications to have on hand. It is difficult to have to run out and get applications copied once people start to come in.

---

[6] Exhibit 5

✓ Set up your file folders for each completed application. Or, you can set up a folder for each letter of the alphabet to place applications in alphabetical order.

✓ Let your current tenants know that you are holding an Open House in their building. You should inform them to expect extra foot traffic in the building that day or evening. Extra precaution should be taken to ensure that areas not accessible to the public (occupied apartments, basement, garage, etc.) are kept closed and/or locked during the time period.

✓ If you are renting two apartments in the same building, set up in the apartment closest to the street traffic, with the front apartment doors open.

✓ Set up a small table and two chairs. This is where applicants can complete a rental application if they so desire. Keep the rental applications yourself, so they have to come to you for one. Have some index cards or your business cards available where you can give out your telephone number. This way, if a rental applicant needs to give you additional information not on the application, he or she can call you.

✓ Make up a sign indicating the amount of the rent, and if any utilities must be paid by the tenant. Make up a second sign indicating what you intend to verify on the rental application. If you charge for application processing, put that amount on the sign. Tell whether or not the unit is de-leaded.

Give Full Disclosure of Apartment Use

Your third sign should tell applicants what they can and cannot do in the apartment[7]. You don't want to pick your perfect tenant, only to find that he or she will not take the apartment because you don't allow pets or she can't have a washing machine. Some rules could be deal breakers for a rental applicant. The sign should indicate your house rules, such as:

- Can the tenant use the building driveway or garage?

- If there is storage space in the building, can your tenant use it?

- Can your tenant remove the brown paneling you installed in the master bedroom, and paint the walls?

- Can your tenant use the back yard for picnics? Can their children play in the yard?

- Can the tenant install a swing set or basketball post in the back yard?

- Can the tenant install a satellite dish?

- Can the tenant install a washing machine and dryer in the apartment? If yes, who will pay for the plumbing installation?

---

[7] Exhibit 1

- Can the tenant paint over or replace the bedroom wallpaper?

You should be as up front as possible about how you want your apartment used by a tenant. Specific restrictions as outlined in this chapter should be added to the lease to ensure that there is an understanding of your requirements. Do not lead them on, or let them assume that they have full access or control if in reality, you want to maintain the apartment a certain way. This will avoid animosity and charges of misrepresentation by your tenant later on in the tenancy.

You may want to show your finalists a copy of the lease, especially if you have added special clauses or restrictions, which may impact the applicant's decision to continue the application process. Better to find out now than when you have made a selection and are ready to give out the keys.

This kind of information may seem unnecessary. However, there are many owners who are supremely territorial with their property, and have restrictions on its use by tenants. I have managed properties where the tenants were not allowed to do anything on the above list. Giving out this type of information in advance will save you and the candidate a lot of time. You will also save money by not processing an application that will not result in a rental. If a person knows in advance that he cannot have his pit bull dog in the apartment, he will not complete a rental application.

Once you put the signs up, you should not enter into any discussion or negotiations with an applicant. Let the signs speak for themselves. You do not want to discuss a change in your rules with a potential applicant, when you do not even know if that person will pass your process. Also, if another applicant overhears you negotiating, he or she could try to do the same thing.

Showing The Apartment

You may not want to open your entire building up to a lot of strangers at an Open House. You may decide if there has been a low number of applicant responses, to show the vacant apartment as applicants call you.

Be sure to tell the applicant which floor the vacant apartment is on. If the applicant will need assistance in seeing the apartment, the two of you should discuss the particulars. For example, how will an applicant who uses a wheelchair get to see the third floor apartment? Federal law states that you cannot refuse to rent or show the third floor apartment to a disabled person. Therefore, you need to discuss how the applicant can see the unit. Ask if the person can bring someone to assist him or her.

Show up on time for your own appointments. This way, you can see if the applicant shows up on time, or is late. Bring a rental application and verification forms with you in a folder set up for the applicant's paperwork.

Make sure you have the right keys to the apartment. There is nothing more frustrating than driving all the way to a building, only to find out the keys do not work. Label your keys if you have more than one vacancy. Put a copy of the entry door key on each vacancy key ring, so you don't have to try to keep up with two sets of keys.

If you decide only one person will show the apartment, this course of action must be planned. We live in an imperfect society. Whether man or woman, you need to be aware and accept the fact that not all applicants may be legitimate. Certain safety precautions should be used.

You need to think about how you will accommodate applicants with physical disabilities. Especially if the vacant apartment is not on the first floor level, you need to make arrangements for applicants to be able to see the unit. You cannot refuse to show an apartment to a person who needs assistance to see it. Ask if the person plans to bring someone to help them navigate the stairs.

If the applicant requests that you go to their current apartment to complete the rental application, do it. If the applicant lives too far away to drive, make arrangements to mail the application to the person. Include all needed verification forms in the package.

Precaution - Bring someone with you when:

o You show the apartment after work hours or after dark;
o The property is in a secluded area;
o No one else is in the building at the time;
o More than two people will be looking at the apartment;

Take notice of:

❖ Who the applicant brings to the apartment with him or her. A boyfriend or girlfriend may end up living there one day;

❖ Whether or not the kids are allowed to run around the apartment at will. If this is how they are allowed to behave when it is important to give a good impression, the parents may have a discipline problem;

❖ Whether or not the applicant is flirting with you. These things happen, ladies and gentlemen. The applicant may be trying to gain an extra edge to your decision making process. Even if the applicant looks like one of the 50 Most Beautiful People in People Magazine, keep to your business. You have nothing to worry about as long as you stick to the facts, and stay away from the fiction.

Be interested in the applicant, but do not try to get too friendly. There are owners who try to develop a relationship too soon into the process. This could color your perception of the applicant during the verification process. If you get too attached to the applicant at the beginning, you may try to justify questionable or negative information about the applicant to your detriment later on.

Keep questions and comments on a business level. Do not let an applicant into your personal life with questions about how long you have had or managed the property, why you bought it, and so on. Questions and answers should be limited to the renting of the apartment and whether or not the applicant is interested in it.

Give the applicant a tour of the entire apartment. Point out or demonstrate any special amenities about the apartment such as ceiling fans, a back porch, or a new stove. Then let the applicant walk around the apartment on his or her own. Don't follow him or her around like a shadow. Give the applicant breathing room to absorb the atmosphere, look into closets, and generally get a feel for the unit. Applicants have to imagine living there, and it's a little difficult when there is another person following them around. If there is a question, you can go into the room to answer it.

Be careful not to oversell the apartment, the building, or the neighborhood. If you make statements like, "this building has state-of-the-art security equipment", or "our keys cannot be duplicated', you may open yourself up to a future lawsuit. You never know what can go wrong in the future. Let the apartment and the building speak for itself as much as possible.

If an applicant wants to know if the building is 'safe', or if there have been a lot of break-ins in the building, I give them the facts. I will tell them how many, if any, break-ins have happened at the property over a period of years. I may say, "We had two break-ins over the past three years. One was questionable, because there was no damage to the apartment lock. The other break-in had no explanation. We put an extra lock on each apartment door to try to address the problem".

I tell an applicant that I do not and cannot guarantee a 'safe' or 'secure' building. I tell them what the history of the property has been, and what has been done to prevent or minimize breaches of security, if any has occurred. An owner or manager cannot control everything on a piece of real estate. I will let an applicant know that the current tenants are diligent about keeping the entry doors closed at all times.

I tell an applicant that I frown on people who leave the building without making sure the front door is closed shut. I also tell the applicant that I expect the tenant's family and friends to do the same. I tell an applicant that security is the responsibility and duty of every person who lives in the building. The building is only as secure as each person who lives there behaves toward the property.

Some applicants will ask if they can change the color of a room, or add something to the apartment, such as a 220 electrical plug. Be specific with your response. Tell them if they will have permission if they are selected, and under what conditions. Who will pay for the extra plugs? Who will install the extra plugs? Will their requested changes to the apartment affect the amount of rent the tenant will have to pay? Make sure to disclose which alterations and/or additions will have to remain on the property when they leave, and which changes can be taken with them. For example, if they want to install ceiling fans or mini blinds, they become a permanent part of the apartment, and have to stay when they leave.

Write these special request items down on the rental application. You do not want to forget what the applicant asked for, and how you responded. You will be looking at a lot of applications, and each person may have different requests for the apartment. Jot them down right away, and do not depend on your memory.

Make sure each person has read the policy and procedure signs. Give out a rental application to those who decide to go to the next step. Ask him or her to fill it out, or as much as possible, if they are interested in renting the unit. If they cannot finish it, at least you will have enough information to call them later. You need the rental application because it is your policy, and to write down their questions and your answers.

Let the person know who is the final decision maker about renting out the apartment. Let them know also who gets to decide about their special requests, if any. Even if you are the owner, maintain your objectivity. If you say yes too soon, you may compromise yourself later if you find out what is asked for will cost you a lot of extra cash. Let the person know that their requests will be considered again if they are selected for the apartment.

Working with a Broker

How many people does it take to rent an apartment? It depends on how fast you want it rented. It depends on whether or not you feel you have the expertise, or even the time, to get the apartment rented quickly, with a good tenant.

I have had several people show up at my open houses that I later discovered were real estate brokers with their clients. Later, if their client indicated they wanted the apartment, the broker would contact me and try to make a deal. Indicate on one of the signs whether or not brokers are welcome. You should know in advance if you want to hire a broker, or fill the unit yourself.

A real estate broker is licensed to represent an owner to complete real estate transactions. A written agreement must be in place between a broker and the building owner. Broker fees for finding a tenant range from one half to a full month's rent.

Again, this is not the time to play it cheap and try to use a friend or relative just starting out as a broker to rent your apartment. You need a person with experience renting out an apartment. The broker should have and use a selection process in the course of their business, just as you would if you were renting out your vacancy yourself. Ask the broker to explain their renting policies and procedures to you before making a hiring commitment.

If you decide to hire a real estate broker, get your money's worth. Let the real estate broker do all of your legwork for you. If applicants contact you directly, give them the name of your broker to contact. This will keep the lines of communication clear. Before you sign any agreement, ask to see his or her license. Make sure the broker has a time line as to when you want the unit rented out. Make sure the broker has a copy of your selection criteria or that he/she understands the parameters.

Make sure you have a good understanding with the broker as to what you want checked, and that you want to see all verified information yourself when it comes in. You want to see *all* of the verification information the broker has completed, because when you pick a person, the result will be your burden to accept and bear. Remember, the broker is interested in making the sale to get paid. Getting the right person for you is not always the primary concern on the broker's agenda. It is *your responsibility* as the owner or manager of the property.

Chapter 5

Rental Tactics That Could Mean Trouble

Homeowners who rent their own apartments have established their own way of marketing and leasing their units. These methods have worked for them for years. However, today's rental applicants are smarter, more astute, and creative, with their own marketing techniques. Some applicants can project an image they believe you desire, and change their behavior as soon as they get the key to your building.

An owner needs to be knowledgeable about fair housing and discrimination laws in the state where the housing is located. Failure to follow the city, state, and federal housing laws could get you in trouble. Even more, it could cost you thousands of dollars in legal fees and fines.

Here are some rental tactics I believe no longer work, and I believe should not be used today. Consider yourself lucky if you can still get away with finding good tenants by using these methods.

For additional information on prohibited renting practices as covered by the Federal Fair Housing Acts, go to Chapter 13 on Fair Housing Laws.

"I have a good feeling about this family"

One should never lease a rental property *solely* based on the warm and fuzzy feeling the applicant gives out. A vacant apartment is a financial real estate investment. Even if your mortgage is paid off, you still want to cover your basic building expenses. You want to be comfortable with the stranger or group of strangers about to live in your home or building. Your intuition should never be a substitute for sound research and verification of all the facts of your applicant's information.

"She needs a place to stay. I'd like to help her out"

You are not running a charity or a shelter. Renting out a vacant apartment is a business. Money is exchanged each month for rental space. The phrase 'no good deed is returned unpunished' means that you may be renting your apartment out of good will. But when something goes wrong in the apartment, or the rent does not get paid, both parties will revert to business owner and customer. Stick to your tenant selection plan, and let those who have not read this book do their good deed with their apartment.

"He seems to be a nice young man looking for his first apartment"

Don't get sidetracked by an applicant's flattery. This is not a personality contest. "Never judge a book by its cover" is still good sound advice. He may look good in his clothes, but that could be because he spends all of his money on clothes and short changes on rent. You want to know if he pays his bills, how much he makes, and how long he has held a job. How old is he? Why is this his first apartment? Where has he been living for the past five years? These are the concrete pieces of information you want and need to know.

"Graduate students are always stable"
"Section 8 Tenants are all bad"
"Section 8 Tenants are all good"

You should not classify any group of applicant as 'better' than another. You will find that no one group of applicant has a monopoly on being either all good or bad.

You are in business to make money from your rented apartment(s). Don't exclude possibly good candidates because of prejudice, negative stereotype casting, or even past bad experiences you may have had. Every person is unique to his or herself. Judge candidates by their rental application and your selection process criteria.

More importantly, if you discriminate against any person or persons of a protected class, such as race, color, national origin, sex, religion, disability/handicap, or familial[8] status, you could open yourself up to a lawsuit. Put your personal issues aside, and work to find the most qualified, rent paying tenant.

"I've been doing this a long time. I know how to pick good tenants "

That may have been true at one point in your life. Times have changed, and people are not always as honest or forthright as they used to be. There are those who do not have respect for other people's property, and have enjoyed going from one building or neighborhood to another for

---

[8] Familiar status is the family composition, such as unwed mother, single parent with children, single man, etc.

years. They are experts at deception and getting around tenant selection processes.

Laws have changed as well. You may discover there are things you can no longer say or do while interviewing a rental applicant. Fair housing testers hired by the U.S. Department of Housing and Urban Development are always on the lookout for owners, brokers and managers who rent out or withhold apartments in violation of state and/or federal laws.

"Word of mouth is always the best way to get an apartment rented"

There is no one perfect way to find the best tenant for an apartment. Word of mouth, though, will always get applicants knocking at your door.

"I know her mother. She's a very nice, reliable, trustworthy person"

However, her daughter may be the worse housekeeper in town, or has a poor rent paying history. Do not rent your apartment based on a person who will not live in your building. Every person has to stand on his or her own merit. You will avoid the disappointment of having to tell her mother you are evicting her daughter for excessive repairs, or non-payment of rent, or a host of other possible reasons.

"I don't want to rent to families with children. I'll tell them the apartment has lead paint."

You cannot try to discourage a rental applicant from applying for your apartment by giving them incorrect or misleading information that would cause the person or persons to look elsewhere.

In some states, the fact that your apartment has lead paint does not prevent you from renting the vacant apartment to an applicant. In states such as Massachusetts, if an applicant still wants to rent the apartment from you, not only must you consider the application, but you must also de-lead the apartment before moving in the tenant.

You need to check the laws in your state concerning lead paint prevention and rental practices.

"I don't want to rent to ... (applicants on welfare, minorities, Section 8 applicants, families with children, etc.).

"They look like they can't afford my rent. I'll tell them the apartment is rented"

"They have really young children. I'll tell them the rent is $100 more per month than I've told the other rental applicants"

You can't open your vacancy door to get applicants, and close it when certain people walk through it. This is considered discriminatory behavior, and a violation of the Federal Fair Housing Acts. You cannot refuse to provide a rental application to or refuse to deal with applicants in specific classes provided by federal law. Furthermore, if you are caught trying not to rent with specific rental applicants, you can be sued and/or fined by both the federal and state governments.

This means you cannot tell black applicants that you rented your vacancy, and tell white applicants that the apartment is still available. You cannot tell your property management company to give preferential treatment to Hispanics or Asians, nor can you behave that way.

For more specific information, see Chapter 13 on Fair Housing Laws.

"All I need to do is find a person who really needs an apartment, and who will agree to fix it up in exchange for the first month's rent"

My motto in an area like this is "How you begin is how you will end". If you have your tenant do repair work in exchange for the first month's rent, that is the first and a lasting impression that person or persons will have of you as a landlord. No matter how many years they stay in the apartment, they will always remember that they had to fix up 'your apartment' when they moved in. It is not a good way to begin a landlord-tenant relationship.

Also, there is invariably the discussion as to what was done, whether or not it was done "correctly", and the final value, if any, to the repair work. If the work was done great, the applicant will take ownership of whatever was done. That may include the installation of a ceiling fan while he or she was fixing and painting the ceiling. If the work was done poorly, you may decide you want to charge the tenant for the workmanship to be done over, especially at security deposit return time.

Either way, there will be an argument, and fond memories and goodwill will fall out the door in trying to negotiate closure. If the matter gets to court, the tenant will have the opportunity to tell the judge that the apartment was not ready for occupancy when the first month's rent was paid. The tenant will portray himself or herself as 'doing the landlord a favor' (which will be true), and you could find yourself defending your motives then and later.

To the extent possible, have the apartment fixed up and completely ready for occupancy before the tenant moves in. If this is not possible, arrange to have your repair people go in and take care of any outstanding items within ten days of the move-in date. Use the first month's rent to pay your contractors.

Do not forget to complete an Apartment Inspection Form before the tenant moves in, preferably with the tenant, and get their signature. When the rest of the repairs are completed, staple a copy of the invoices to your inspection form and keep it in the tenant's folder for future reference. When or if the return of the security deposit comes into question, you will be able to not only prove the original condition of the apartment when you turned it over to your tenant, but to show that the repairs were completed within a reasonable time span.

"I don't usually rent out my apartments without doing a credit check, but this applicant clearly had money"

Your applicant drives a BMW, has a Coach purse, always wears expensive, form fitting clothes, works for IBM, and currently lives in an upscale neighborhood. Yes, the applicant did indeed have money. Unfortunately, she had just enough to pay the first, last month's rent, and the security deposit. The reality of the situation is that so much money goes into her material goods that her credit report looks like the Who's Who of impending bankruptcy court. The real reason why she is looking for another apartment is that she can no longer afford where she now lives, and her creditors are closing in on her.

The point here is, do not make exceptions when you are processing rental applications. Complete the entire process from beginning to end, regardless of an applicant's outward appearance. What lurks behind that "good tenant" façade could be a multitude of sins that you will end up paying for in eviction court costs.

"I don't care what anybody says. This is my building, and I have to live here. I'm going to rent it the way I see fit, and to whom I want"

These are what I call Famous Last Words. Good luck.

The 19th century writer Henry David Thoreau once said, "It is never too late to give up your prejudices." This is why you need this book. Hopefully, if you prepare a Tenant Selection Plan that is based on fair play, good faith, and adherence to the law, we won't have to see you in court.

Chapter 6

The Rental Application

Y ou should use a rental application that comes from a legal entity or organization that has had their rental application reviewed by an attorney. Your local real estate board usually has copies of rental applications for sale. Or, you should have your attorney recommend a rental application form to you. It is considered a legal document, in that the applicant is certifying that what he or she has written on it is true to the best of their knowledge. You are relying on that information as the primary basis for making your renting decisions. Unless you are an attorney expert in real estate law, leave the writing of this document to those who are certified to know your state laws regarding tenancies.

Insist that *every applicant* complete a rental application. Even friends and relatives should complete one. It makes it easier to compare information. You will also not have to try to remember what the applicant said to you about employment, income, etc. When you speak with the applicant, you can jot down notes on the rental application.

If the applicant is hesitant to fill out an application, take note. If the applicant refuses to fill out an application, inform the person that you will not be able to consider him or her for the apartment.

Make sure that the applicant signs and dates the application. If there is a husband and wife, or roommates, boyfriend and girlfriend, companions, have both or all of them sign the application on the same page. Even if more than one application needs to be completed in the case of non-married applicants, have the other initial next to the applicant's signature. It will remind you that there is more than one person applying to live together in the apartment.

Never refuse to give out a rental application. It is discrimination if you give out a rental application as part of your selection process, yet refuse to give one out to an individual because you don't like their looks, attitude, etc. Take the completed application, and deal with the facts along with all of the others.

Make sure you can read what has been written on the rental application. Go over it with the applicant after it has been completed to make sure you understand what has been written. Otherwise, when you want to confirm a former landlord for example, you will have to call the rental applicant to decode his or her name for you.

Verify all of the information written on the rental application. Failure to check even one piece of information could cause you to make an error in your final decision.

Always process more than one rental application at a time. You never know at which point an applicant will have a problem, or will withdraw his or her application. At least three applications should be verified at the same time for every single vacant apartment. If one doesn't make the cut, you still have two more applications already in process.

When you review the application, make sure the applicants are of legal age to sign a lease. Check the legal age to enter into a contract with your local real estate board. Note that an "emancipated minor" is a person under the age of 18 years who has been granted legal status under the state court system. Have the applicant provide you with a copy as proof he or she can sign a lease and be legally bound by one.

The Information Release Form

In order to get information on the rental applicant's personal business, you need written permission from the applicant. The best way to get this is to attach a Release Form[9] to the back of the rental application. It can then be copied and sent with each written verification form you mail out. Also, if you verify information over the telephone, send a copy of the applicant's release form to the person giving you the information in question.

A general release statement should also be included in the rental application itself. When you purchase a rental application, see if there are disclaimers at the end of the document.

A co-signer should always sign an Information Release form, so that you can verify income, employment, and credit information.

---

[9] Exhibit 3

Carolyn Gibson

<u>Chapter 7</u>

Signs There May Be a Problem, and How to Respond

When your applicant begins to make a series of excuses why he or she cannot comply with your requests, you need to probe deeper and ask follow up questions. The signs are *always* there that you could have a problem applicant. Sometimes we ignore them because everything else about the applicant appears to be okay. Other times, we are in such a hurry to get the unit back on a rent paying basis, we go ahead and rent to the person anyway.

Here are a few examples of questions from rental applicants that should cause you to examine further.

"Why do I Have to fill out an application?"

Uh-oh, we have a difficult applicant, and so it begins. And, guess what? This question will most likely come from one of your closet friends or relative. Do not start your vacancy process by playing favorites or catering to those who do not want to follow the rules.

Everyone should fill out a rental application, regardless of his or her status with you. Not only is it part of fair housing legislation in many states, it is the best way to treat everyone as equal. Also, if you receive a number of applications for one unit, you will appreciate being able to have something in writing to review and compare information from one candidate to another.

Make everyone go through the process from beginning to end. Your favorite cousin may owe everyone in town. Your life long friend may have a criminal record he or she is not proud to reveal. Tell them you are making everyone do the same thing, to keep things honest and equal.

Here is the definitive reason why everyone should fill out a rental application: *It is your policy, your property, and your rules*. It is a business renting out your apartment on a month-to-month basis and receiving rent money to lease it. If they do not have a problem giving a credit card company or a car company their personal business to get credit, they should not have a problem filling out a rental application to get an apartment. They have no problem at all filling out an employment application. Your apartment is at the same level of business.

"My mother (father, aunt, sister, etc.) said that I wouldn't have to go through the regular process"

This is an example of what can happen when you tell your friend or relative you have a vacant apartment to rent. The presumption is that you will give preferential treatment. Not true. Let your friends and relatives know that you are serious about your apartment and building. If you begin a tenancy by not following your own policies and procedures, they will remind you of that fact when there is a problem later.

"I need an apartment for next month"

Whoa. Slow Down. Beware the applicant in a hurry. You want to get the apartment rented as quickly as possible. Still, do not allow yourself to be rushed through your own verification process by an applicant rushing you.

There are applicants who are very good at imposing their "emergency situation" on an owner or manager. Especially if an applicant has children, they can encourage an owner or manager to rent to the applicant before all of the paperwork and verifications are completed. The owner or manager subsequently may find that the "emergency situation" was actually an impending eviction. But too late - now the tenant is in your apartment.

"I didn't bring my glasses with me. I have to come back"

This could happen often, especially with older applicants. They may not have expected to have to complete an application for the apartment right then and there at the Open House. Or, it might be possible that the applicant saw your application requirements on the wall, and knew he or she could not pass the process. This is a dignified way for an applicant to back out. Let him or her go, without taking an application. If eyeglasses are really needed, the applicant will come back, or ask for your telephone number for another appointment date.

"I don't have all my information with me. Can I take the application with me?"

There are different schools of thought regarding whether or not you should let your rental application out of your control. My thought is to keep your applications with you, so that you can keep track of them, how many you have, how many you gave out, etc. If they are serious about the apartment, they should be prepared to complete it then. They can always come back with their additional information. Sometimes the person may be illiterate, or have a reading problem. Older applicants may need their reading glasses to fill it out. Help each applicant who indicates he or she needs it.

Beware the applicant that is surprised he or she has to fill out an application at all. Most small landlords do not use a written process. There are bad risk applicants that depend on being able to talk their way into getting an apartment. Always use a rental application to lease your units.

"I intend to pay three months of rent in advance if I am selected"

When was the last time anyone has *ever* paid the rent three months in advance, along with the security deposit? Your response should be to remind the applicant that you still have to complete the tenant selection process on the rental application before you make a final decision. Also, you have more than one application under consideration.

There are people who will try to take advantage of your eagerness to rent your apartment so that you can start to get money to help pay the mortgage. Do not allow a rental applicant to wave money in your face to get you to change or rush through your process. Does the application and bank account statement confirm that he or she has this much money? What happens after the three months?

"I want to put a deposit on the apartment in case I am selected"

This is offered by an applicant in order to gain a competitive advantage for the apartment. Again, do not give into money waved in your face. If the candidate is selected through your process, all you want is for the person to pay the rent every month, and obey the rules of the lease. I do not recommend that taking application deposits should be made part of your policy. The record keeping of monies received, and keeping these funds in a separate bank account is an additional responsibility.

If you accept application processing fees, pre-selection checks or money orders and put them in an envelope, now you have other people's money in your home. Some applicants cannot afford to pay an application fee. Some states do not allow owners to take an application fee or deposit. Check the law in your state before you accept any processing fee money.

Can the Applicant Afford the Rent?

Let us suppose that after your open house, you have collected 15 or more rental applications. Each application should be reviewed for financial eligibility. In other words, before you begin to put time and money into processing a rental application, you should determine whether or not the applicant can afford your rent. This is vastly different from whether or not the applicant has the rent and all of the security deposit ready and in hand *now* if he or she is selected for the apartment.

Let's say that you have a vacant two-bedroom apartment that you wish to rent for $800 per month, with no utilities included. You have determined that the average monthly electric, gas and heating bills come to an additional $350 per month. The actual gross rent for the apartment is therefore $1,150.

You have to include in your calculations the utility bills that the tenant will have to pay. This is a monthly expense that the tenant will have to pay in addition to the rent, so it must be factored as part of the total rent package. Many times I have heard from a tenant that the heat bill in the

Carolyn Gibson

apartment was extra high for a month, causing him or her to be late paying the rent.

Therefore, you must add the average utility bill to the rent in determining the applicant's ability to pay everything that comes with the apartment. To do this, you divide the annual gross (before taxes) income of every person expected to pay the rent by twelve. Subtract certain standard dependent deductions, and such deductions as child-care expenses if applicable. Then multiply that amount by the percentage of income you think is appropriate for an applicant to be able to afford your apartment. For example:

Annual Gross Income	$ 45,000
Subtract $480 for each child[10] Two children, ages 4 and 6 years	$ 960
Subtract Annual Child Care Expenses $74 per week[11] x 2 children, for 50 weeks	$ 7,400
Divide $ 36,640 by 12 Adjusted Month Income	$ 3,053
Multiply by percentage of income (40%) Amount of rent the tenant can pay each month	$ 1,221 =

After deducting for mandatory expenses, the applicant can minimally afford to pay the $1,150 rent each month. The remainder of their income will go for basic living expenses, and optional expenses, such as car, credit cards,

---

[10] Standard Section 8 deduction

[11] Child Care Bureau, Administration for Children and Families, U.S. Department of Health & Human Services, Child Care Bulletin, September/October 1997, Issue 17, White House Conference on Child Care

etc. This would be a tight situation for the applicant. There is no extra cushion room. It could work if the applicant were currently paying more than 40% of rent, and renting your apartment would lower that cost.

Why did I use 40% of the applicant's income? It could and should be any number lower than fifty percent. The federal government allows a Section 8 tenant to pay 30% of his or her income for rent. The remaining 70% is paid to the landlord by the federal government in the form of a voucher payment. To determine a market rate applicant's ability to pay rent, the industry standard is a bit higher. I usually work around the 40% mark as the *maximum* income to rent ratio.

When reviewing an applicant's ability to pay, you should factor in what the applicant is currently paying for rent. You can also use lower numbers for monthly utility costs, if you know your average utility bills. Utilities may not actually cost $350 per month, depending on the geographic location of the property.

Let us follow this calculation for another example. The same two-bedroom apartment is available for $800 per month. This time, the applicant will only have to pay an average monthly electrical bill of $75, totaling $875 per month. The applicant has one child.

Annual Gross Income	$45,000
Subtract $480 for each child A sixteen year old son	480
Subtract Child Care Expenses	$ 0
Divide $44,520 by 12 Adjusted Monthly Income	$ 3,710
Multiply by percentage of income (40%) Amount of rent the tenant can pay each month	$ 1,484 =

81

Clearly, the applicant can afford to pay $875 per month for rent at 40% of her income for rent. In fact, this applicant would only have to pay 23.5% of her income toward rent.

What you are actually looking for is an amount of income that will allow a tenant to pay the rent with ease each month. There is not an exact science in determining ability to pay. You have to factor in several pieces of information, such as, how long has she been paying this kind of rent? Can the applicant afford to pay this rent by himself? How many credit cards is he or she paying in addition to the rent?

If you talk to most landlords and property managers, they like to keep the ratio between income and rent at thirty five percent. Still, I have often been asked if I have ever accepted a rental applicant who would pay higher than thirty five percent of his or her income for rent. Yes, in instances where the applicant is currently paying for example, forty percent or higher for rent, and is looking for a cheaper place to live. Clearly, if the applicant has been successfully paying forty two percent of his or her gross income for rent for the past five years, has good credit and no rent delinquencies, all other factors considered, I would regard this applicant a relatively good risk paying forty percent of income for rent.

There are many owners who do not calculate ability to pay by a percentage. The normal calculation for many owners is to calculate the gross income times the rent. This calculation is done without taking away deductions for childcare, utilities, etc. In other words, if the monthly rent is $800, a landlord will want to see an applicant who makes 2 ½ times $800, or $2,000 per month gross income. Some owners want to see a three-time ratio between income and rent. If the monthly rent is $800, the owner will require that the applicant make $2,400 gross income per month, or three times the monthly rent.

In calculating income to rent ratios, you do not want to cut too close to the ratio between an applicant's ability to pay and the rent. You need to review whether or not the applicant has a cushion of income to fall back on in case of an emergency. You also want to enable an applicant to pay any rent increase you may need to impose at a future date. If an applicant is barely making it at 40% of their adjusted income, a rent increase may push their ability to pay to the limit.

Look at the entire application when determining ability to pay. If the applicant has a good-sized savings account, this can be used to cover rent during a crisis. If an applicant has been working at the same job for three or more years, chances are that he or she will receive a pay increase, or even a promotion. Ability to pay is a judgment call for an owner, based on every aspect of information in the rental application.

The Applicant Intimidation Factor

Occasionally, there are signs your applicant could mean future trouble. There are definite signs that perhaps you should take a pass on a person. In addition to the areas discussed in this chapter, you should think about the kind of relationship you would have with the hopeful person if:

- He or she questions every decision or part of the process;

- Every discussion becomes a debate between what you are doing regarding your process, and what he or she thinks you should be doing;

- He or she tries to rush you through the process despite telling him or her repeatedly you will get back to him or her when you have completed the application;

- The applicant appears to have a short temper;

- The applicant makes you feel nervous when around you;

- He or she doesn't want to give you information you have a legal right to have to make informed decisions;

- You feel severely intimidated by the applicant because he or she tends to yell or raise his/her voice when he/she hears something they do not like, or, stands over you or very close to you when making a point or, points his or her finger in your face when talking, etc.

- You smell alcohol on the applicant's breath each time you meet;

I call these intimidation factors that, regardless of whether or not the applicant is doing it on purpose or unconsciously, will cause me to think twice about the candidate. I want a tenancy period over a number of years that will be free from stress, questioning of my authority or rules, and constant bickering. If the applicant and I aren't getting along before I even complete the process, it will not get better after he or she moves in.

You should make a note of the date and time you have these types of encounters with an applicant, and include it in their file folder. Then, when it comes time to decide between one applicant or another, your notes can remind you of situations in which you felt you and the applicant were not on the same page.

See Chapter 11 on "Rejecting an Applicant" for more information on what to do when you decide that you need to move on to another rental applicant.

Carolyn Gibson

Chapter 8

Processing the Rental Application

The gathering of facts and background information is the backbone of the tenant selection process. The more you know about your rental applicant, the better you can lower the possibility of renting to a high-risk tenant.

To process a rental application means to verify the information the applicant wrote on your rental application form. You will receive several varied answers from the questions asked on the application. The answers will vary from those that make perfect sense, to those that sound as if they were made up from a dream the applicant had one night.

The main point is that you have the right to verify, confirm, question or challenge information provided to you on the rental application. You have the right to accept or reject an applicant based on what has been written, alleged to be true, said, or observed.

Make every applicant play by your rules. Keep control of the entire rental application process. Watch the applicant who brings a relative with him or her to complete the application. Observe which person takes control of the process from the applicant's end. For example, if an aunt is doing most of the paperwork and most of the communicating, take extra precautions with the applicant. She may be trying to get her niece or nephew out of her apartment for a good reason.

I rented a unit to an applicant with a very diligent aunt. She was personable, talkative, and very interested in the entire application process. I mistook her extreme interest in the verification process for good family concern. I asked why her nephew could not contribute to his own application process, she replied that he was 'slow', and needed help. He did appear to need assistance, so I left it at that. Both appeared eager to do whatever was needed to obtain an apartment for the nephew.

It turned out that the nephew, who was living with his aunt at the time, had been evicted from several apartments, until he had ended up at hers. She had arranged to have the nephew move out of every former unit on his own, so there was no eviction record in court or on his credit report for owing rent. The aunt had all of his paperwork in order, and so I thought, here is a good applicant, with strong family back up for support.

Wrong! The minute the nephew moved in, the aunt disappeared. He allowed every ne'er do well in his apartment, and the parties and drug taking went on non-stop. Appeals to the aunt went unheeded, and we ended up in eviction court. The aunt returned, moved out her nephew, again, before the court process could be completed.

The situation could have been avoided by checking all of the past landlord references, in hope that at least one of them would give us the real story. We could have interviewed the nephew more instead of allowing the aunt to control the process. We learned that when an applicant is too eager to cooperate, we should take a little more time checking out reference information.

Sometimes, a landlord will allow a person to rush their application, especially if money is tight. Make sure that you apply the same rules to every applicant. If he or she can't wait until you finish processing the application, it doesn't matter how much money they make. There is a problem somewhere. If the applicant is in a hurry, let them put their stuff in storage until you complete the process. You cannot guarantee or commit the person an apartment until you have finished processing the application.

Why do I have to go through so much trouble?

The more you pre-screen a rental applicant, the lower the risk of making a poor choice of tenant. If all you want is to fill your vacant apartment and get the first month's rent in the bank, any process will suffice. If you want to have a tenant that will stay a long time, respect your property, respect the neighbors, and pay the rent on time every month, something more than a money order, three pay stubs and a letter from the current landlord is required.

You want to not only have a good tenant in your home or building. You want to be repaid for all the money you have invested into your vacant apartment. The longer your tenant stays and pays the rent every month, the sooner you will get your money back. The cost of making repairs and verifying all of the applicant's information is repaid by the positive, long-term occupancy of your apartment. The cost of cutting corners, time and money could cost you legal fees, extensive repairs to the apartment as well as the building, and even the reputation of your building.

Why do you want to know so much about a rental applicant? Why spend from $75 to $150 per person checking so much background information? After all, you don't want to become a private detective just to fill a vacant apartment.

Why do you want to verify every piece of information given to you by your rental applicant? Let's look at an example situation by assuming you rented your two bedroom apartment recently without the benefit of a credit check or other checks. The tenant has been in the apartment for about seven months, and has not paid the rent for the month. You now have to go through the legal process.

Here is a list of average fees an owner would have to pay to evict a non-paying tenant in a two-bedroom apartment:

Lost rent for one month	$800
Attorney Fees	$500
Constable/Sheriff Fees	$175
Court Fees	$150
Lost salary to attend court (based on $45,000 salary)	$173 per day
Lost rent after winning in court	$800
Cost of the eviction truck for a 4 hour minimum[12]	$750

Total Cost of Lost Rent and Eviction   ***$3,348***

You have won your case, even though it cost you a few thousand dollars. Now, let's look at the cost of preparing your new vacant unit. If we make some assumptions about the apartment, look at what you now have to pay to get another tenant.

---

[12] In some states, you are required to also pay for storage of the evicted tenant's belongings for a period of months

One Month's Rent lost while painting and making repairs	$800
Advertising Costs (newspapers, flyers, etc.)	$ 75
Cost of Painting and Repairs	$800
One Month's Rent lost while showing apartment to applicants	$800
Application Processing Fees	$150
Misc. Expenses – Utility bills[13], inspection certificate[14], etc.	$100

Total Cost of Renting a Two Bedroom Vacancy $2,725

Total Cost of Eviction and Re-Renting a Two-Bedroom Unit $6,073

Depending on where you live, these are conservative numbers. The amount of time and lost money usually goes up, depending upon the eviction laws in your state, how long you wait before you start the eviction process, the condition in which the tenant left the apartment, and other relevant factors.

This is not all money that will come out of your pocket, but it is money will you never see again. If we accept the sample time frame above and the dollars lost getting a vacant apartment re-rented, it will take an owner at least eight months of rent to recover expenses lost by a vacant apartment. Do you still want to skip the cost of doing a credit, landlord, eviction, and criminal check on each rental applicant?

---

[13] You will have to keep the utilities on during the vacancy while you are making repairs, painting, etc.

[14] Some states or local ordinances require an owner to pay a fee to have a state inspector certify that the apartment is in compliance with state building codes.

Carolyn Gibson

How much will it cost me in time and money?

You will spend money to process a rental application. How much you spend financially and in time will depend on how much information you have to verify, how fast people respond to your inquiries, etc.

The best way to make sure you verify all of the information on the rental application is to use an Application Processing Checklist form[15]. On the form is a list of all possible information that can be verified. You can check those pieces of information that need to be checked after a review of the rental application information.

How much time does this entire verification-processing take? It depends on how you choose to verify the information, in writing or by telephone, what you decide to verify, how many verifications needed, and the availability of the person or agency from which you need the information. It could take at least a month to a month and a half from beginning to end.

When I managed properties for investment owners, they would ask why I took so long renting their apartments. I will explain the process to them regarding the credit check, landlord check, etc. and how important it is to verify every piece of information on the rental application. At times an owner would tell me I was taking too long, and would ask to cut corners in order to rent out the apartments at a faster pace.

As I would be the same person who would have to evict a high-risk tenant I accepted, I knew I would have a similar

---

[15] See Exhibit 4

conversation with the owner regarding the high legal fees incurred to get the tenant out of the apartment.

The cost and the time of processing a rental application will pale in the face of an even bigger potential problem, which is the aggravation of moving out a tenant. Think of the expense of hiring an attorney, the time you will have to put in the eviction case, and the money you will have to pay to remove the tenant from your apartment and get it ready for another family. Think of the stress and anxiety of doing all of this at the same time you are trying to go to work every day, and raise your own family.

It may seem convenient to put someone in your apartment that initially seems to be a good candidate. Still, when a landlord-tenant relationship goes bad, you will look back at all the things you should or could have done when you were interviewing the applicant. The cost of processing a rental application or even several will appear minimal when you find yourself in the throes of an expensive eviction case that seems to go on forever.

Don't put yourself on the wrong side of the 'pay me now, or pay me later' syndrome. Even if things go wrong at a later date, you will find some comfort in knowing that you did everything possible to ensure that you chose the right person or family for your apartment. Take the time and spend the money at the front of the process, and it could minimize your expenses, time and frustration at the end of the process.

Who Should I Check Out?

You should check out every person who will pay the rent, whether in part or in total. Each person must sign a release form giving you permission to do a credit check.

Get the social security number of every person in the household. Most children have one as well as the adults. Some parents put their utility bills in the name of their children. You need to see if the children have poor credit reports because of unpaid utility or telephone bills. Have the parents sign a release form on behalf of their children so you can do a credit check.

The Credit Check

Checking the rental applicant's credit is one of the most critical pieces of information necessary. With the inclusion of verifying income, you must know whether or not the applicant has the ability to pay the rent along with their other bills. Look to see if the applicant is overextended with bills, or has neglected to pay back credit cards, automobile loan, student loan, medical bills, etc.

You can understand the applicant's attitude about debt by examining the credit report. Are student loans and medical bills being paid? These bills are just as important as credit cards. By looking at the credit report, you can see what kind of buying habits the applicant has. Also, you will see which bills the applicant considers important enough to pay. Is the car note always paid on time, but there are four credit cards that are always in arrears? Is their student loan overdue?

The credit report may indicate that the applicant has too many financial obligations. A person loaded down in debt may have trouble keeping up with rent payments. Look at:

- How long the applicant has had credit;
- How long the applicant has had each debt, credit card, loan;

- How much total money is still owed by the applicant?
- Has the applicant ever been late paying debts? By how many months?

At the same time, if the applicant has been carrying a large debt and has a good rent payment history, that could be in his or her favor.

If the applicant is in dispute with a creditor, that notation should appear on the credit report. If the report shows a number of disputed bills, you may not want to become one of them at a later date. If the report shows that your applicant has a payment plan for delinquent bills, that indicates the applicant is a responsible person who likes to honor a debt, even if it takes a while to get it cleared up. I consider that type of proactive action to repair credit a big plus for the applicant.

One should always look for a credit bureau with a national database. You want to check whether or not the applicant has lived in another state and did not report that information. With a national database, you can even get information from Puerto Rico, the US. Virgin Islands, and all other Commonwealths of the United States.

What if you look at the credit report and find the applicant has once filed bankruptcy? The red flag should go up. The applicant should be questioned more carefully. Certainly, when and why bankruptcy was filed has to be answered.

These days, you can get the results of a credit check within hours. Do not forget to have the applicant sign a release form indicating their permission for you to get a copy. Also, many credit bureaus are very strict. They do not want you to show the credit report to the applicant. Send your applicants to the credit bureau where you received your information to get their own copy.

How to Read and Interpret a Credit Report

Reading and interpreting a credit report can be tricky. There are many variables to consider. It is actually possible for a person to have a bad credit report, yet also have a spotless rent payment record. There could be a case where a tenant receives a rent increase, and decides to keep up with the rent payments while looking for another apartment, instead of keeping up with credit card bills. You would see the reason for looking for another apartment was a rent increase on their rental application. Find out by how much, and determine how much the rent increase has affected the applicant's ability to pay both bills and the rent.

Credit Bureaus

Equifax	**Experian**	**Trans Union**
P.O. Box 740241	P.O. Box 2104	760 Sproul Road
Atlanta, GA 30374-0241	Allen, TX 75013	P.O. Box 390
		Springfield, PA
		19064-0390
1-800-685-1111	1-888-397-3742	1-800-916-8800

www.Equifax.com
www.experian.com
www.transunion.com

A Bankruptcy Report

Bankruptcy is a way for a person overwhelmed by debt to either re-schedule their payments, or walk away from them all. There are some who believe that a person who has filed for bankruptcy is a deadbeat with a poor attitude about debt, and who should not be given the opportunity to "cheat" an owner out of paying rent. Here is a brief history of bankruptcy in order for you to put this practice in some perspective when reviewing the credit report.

In the Middle Ages of England and Europe, businessmen and other creditors ruled the day where bankruptcy was concerned. Not being able to pay your bills was considered a serious crime. A bankrupt person was considered a criminal and subject to criminal punishment, from debtors prison to the death penalty. It was not until 1542 that the first official bankruptcy law was passed in England under King Henry the Eighth.

When the United States of America was established in 1776, debtor's prisons were still in effect. In fact, this was only one of many laws carried over from Europe and was maintained in the early days of the new democracy. Over the years, as citizens were able to review which laws they wished to continue and which ones they wished to discard, changes were made in how business was conducted. Although debtors' prisons were not abolished until 1841, the United States enacted its first bankruptcy law in 1800. Early bankruptcy laws were established as temporary responses to bad economic conditions.

Today's bankruptcy laws prefer and emphasize rehabilitating individual and corporate debtors and reorganizing debts while under court protection from creditors. The Bankruptcy Reform Act of 1994 created the Chapter 13 law, which encourages individual debtors to reschedule their debts. A Chapter 7 bankruptcy allows individual debtors to dismiss all debts owed, and starts a new credit history.

The point here is that a person who files for bankruptcy should not necessarily be seen as a rental applicant pariah. There are legitimate reasons why someone would need to file for bankruptcy that you may wish to consider. Divorce, illness, an extended unemployment, a failed business are some credible reasons why filing bankruptcy may be necessary. It is a legal remedy for thousands of people.

Questions you may want to ask regarding the bankruptcy are, what did they learn from filing? Are they under a Chapter 13 schedule now? Are they keeping up with their payments? If Chapter 7 was filed, was unpaid rent one of the debts removed? How long ago did they declare bankruptcy?

If a person has filed for bankruptcy, you might want to know if there was a co-signer involved. Did the applicant file for bankruptcy and leave rent and/or damage payments for the co-signer to pay?

The Employment and Other Income Check

You are looking to rent to a person or family who can and will be able to financially afford your apartment for at least three years. The employment verification[16] will help determine if the applicant has a job, and how much he or she makes per week. Three consecutive pay stubs only tells you that the person worked for the past three weeks. They don't tell you how long they have worked at the same location, or whether or not they get regular overtime pay, or have received salary raises over the years.

There are people who will apply for an apartment using two jobs as their source of income. You need to verify how

---

[16] See Exhibit 7

long the applicant has held each job. I have rented to many applicants who held two long-term, part time jobs. I look for employment stability, not necessarily the kind of job a person holds.

Don't let the applicant bring in his or her own employment letter. The employment letter must be returned to you by mail. This is called third party verification.

Savings Account

Check as part of the income verification the bank account information. Some landlords as well as applicants think this goes too far. I make it a required piece of information. You need to know how the rent will be paid if the resident has a financial problem, such as sickness or unemployment. Do they have only enough money to cover the first month's rent and security deposit?

Savings information could be important if the applicant depends on having two jobs to make ends meet. What happens if she gets laid off from one of her jobs? Is the applicant living from paycheck to paycheck? Many do, and are successful at it. Still, does he or she have enough savings to be able to carry the rent?

Have the applicant bring a copy of their Certificate of Deposit, stocks, bonds, etc. if this is their primary source of savings. Also verify savings held at credit unions.

Other Income

These are all reliable sources of regularly paid income:
- Pension or Trust Fund;
- Unemployment Insurance;
- Child Support;

Carolyn Gibson

- Alimony;
- Aid for Dependent Children (AFDC);
- Disability Insurance;
- Student Scholarship or Stipend;
- Social and Supplemental Security

The key is to ensure the security of other income. Have the applicant sign a release form so that you can confirm these sources of income. Have the applicant give you as much information you need to call or write these agencies.

What you need to know:

✓ Is the child support or alimony court ordered?

✓ Are payments taken from the spouse or significant other's paycheck and sent directly to the applicant?

✓ Does the student have an award letter from the college or university on their letterhead outlining how the funds can be used, or can be used for housing costs?

✓ If receiving unemployment insurance, how many weeks are left for the applicant to receive checks?

✓ Is the disability temporary or permanent?

✓ Is the social security for the applicant or for the minor child(ren)?

✓ If the applicant is an independent contractor, does he receive 1099 income tax forms as proof of income?

The Criminal Record Check

This part of the selection process must be handled with some dignity for the applicant and common sense by the homeowner or manager.

I do not think that you should reject a person with a conviction out of hand. It depends on the nature of the crime, how long ago it happened, what he or she has done with their life since, etc. If a person has paid their debt to society and has stayed free of crime, his or her application should be considered.

At the same time, you want to know that you are not renting your apartment to a convicted child molester, murderer, or other type of person that could be in conflict with your other residents. If, for example, you are renting out a one-bedroom apartment in a building full of young children and/or teenagers, and a convicted double rapist applies for the unit, you might want to take that information into consideration.

You can reject an applicant who is an active illegal drug user, or anyone whose tenancy would interfere with your other tenants rights to the quiet enjoyment of their apartment. You do not have to rent to a person who has been convicted by any court or competent jurisdiction of the illegal manufacture or distribution of illegal drugs.

Information on the criminal history, if any of a rental applicant can be obtained from the credit bureau, a tenant selection form, or your state criminal records department each for a fee.

If you have questions about the criminal record of an applicant, these questions should be answered to your satisfaction. Depending upon the seriousness of the crime, you can either wait until you verify the rest of the rental application information, or you can ask your questions at the Home Visit. There is no issue of confidentiality, because the applicant has either provided this information to you, or has given you permission to get this information on their Release Form[17].

I rented an apartment to a woman with a shop lifting conviction. At the home visit, I asked her if she wanted to discuss it. She was very open about it, saying that at the time, which was a few years before, she had recently been diagnosed with muscular dystrophy, and had a lot of anger about the changes it would have on her life. After she was caught, paid her fine, did her time, and addressed her anger, she never had another problem. I felt that she should not be deprived of an apartment because of this one incident. I also did not feel that she would be a detriment to other tenants in the building. She was one of my best tenants.

At the same time, I did not rent to a gentleman who had been convicted of breaking into his neighbor's apartments to steal their belongings. Even though he did his time and restitution a year before, I did not feel comfortable renting to him under those circumstances.

The Eviction Check

You want to know if your applicant has ever been evicted from an apartment. Second, you need to know why he or she was evicted. Last, you want to know how many

---

[17] Exhibit 3

times, and how long ago the eviction(s) took place. Spend the money on a credit bureau or tenant selection bureau to get this very important piece of rental history.

Sometimes an eviction cannot be helped. For example, if the tenant lost his or her job, went through all savings, and still could not keep up with the rent, an eviction may happen. Perhaps the tenant had a large rent increase put in effect, or is recently divorced, and fell behind in the rent before he or she could find a cheaper apartment. If the eviction was ten years ago, and the candidate has had successful rentals since, I would continue to process the application.

If there is more than one eviction on record, or the applicant was evicted for non-payment of rent and never paid it back, move on to a low-risk application. An owner will always take rent owned to him or her, regardless of how much time passed since a tenant left. If the applicant was evicted for vandalism, late rent payments, or a lease violation, he or she may still be a high-risk applicant, especially if the eviction was recent. You should reject this application if you do not receive a good reason from the applicant about what happened.

The Landlord Check

You need to verify all landlord information given to you in the rental application. You want a referral on the kind of tenant your applicant is or was from the present and past landlord(s). The important thing to remember in this section is that if you do not ask the question, do not expect a rental applicant to volunteer answers.

In addition, the previous landlord may not always tell you the truth. In some cases, a former landlord or manager may have agreed with the local housing court not to give negative information in exchange for the tenant moving out on their own. In other cases, the landlord may want to avoid the former tenant who is trying to solicit a good reference from him or her. The former tenant may also threaten to sue the former landlord if given a bad reference.

What you are looking for is an honest appraisal from the previous landlord as to the positive or negative potential of your rental applicant. Try to get as much information as the landlord or manager is willing to give. Emphasize that the information given will be kept confidential (and keep that commitment).

If the current or previous landlord was a college or university, this should not present a problem. Many students begin their college life in a dormitory, and finish it in an apartment. The college should be able to give you a credible landlord reference with no fear of recrimination. The college is primarily an educational institution, and should not fear repercussions from their students.

Useful Landlord Verification Information from the Department of Housing and Urban Development[18]

Owners may consider extenuating circumstances in evaluating information obtained during the screening process to assist in determining the acceptability of an applicant for tenancy.

EXAMPLE: Through the screening process, an owner learns that Mrs. Smith was evicted from her last apartment for violent and threatening behavior. The owner rejects Mrs. Smith's application and informs her of the reasons for the rejection.

Mrs. Smith explains that her previous behavior was caused by a mental impairment and that she is now receiving the necessary services and daily medication. If the owner has a policy of considering extenuating circumstances for any tenant, the owner would be required to consider the extenuating circumstances applicable to Mrs. Smith.

In evaluating whether to accept Mrs. Smith as a tenant, the owner may verify that these services are being provided and that Mrs. Smith is taking her medication. If the owner learns that Mrs. Smith's current behavior is violent or threatening, as reported to the owner during the screening process, the owner may deny admission to Mrs. Smith in accordance with the tenant selection plan. If the owner does not have a policy of considering extenuating circumstances, s/he is not required to consider such circumstances described by Mrs. Smith.

---

[18] www.hudclips.gov Section 8 Handbook 4350.3

The Landlord doesn't return your calls

This could be a sign that the landlord is unwilling to discuss your applicant's tenancy. Some landlords do not want to get involved. Information provided from one landlord to another is supposed to be confidential. However, there are times when the former tenant can usually figure out who gave a bad reference. And, perhaps the landlord had a bad experience where an owner or manager did not keep what was said or written confidential from the applicant.

There are tenants who will contact their former landlord in advance of applying for another apartment with the goal of intimidating him or her into giving out a good reference. Leave an encouraging message. If you cannot convince a landlord to provide you with a reference, you cannot complete processing the application. Or, depending on whether or not you have other landlord references already in hand, you can make a decision to use what information you have.

The Landlord is on vacation

This is a frustrating situation, when you want to process an application in a hurry, and the person you need to talk to isn't available. Leave a message on the former landlord's answering machine or voice mail. Perhaps he/she will pick up messages while away, and will call you if you express you are on a deadline. In the meantime, you need to move on to another application.

Personal References

I have never depended solely on a personal reference to determine whether or not I would accept an applicant for an apartment. What else is a personal reference suppose to say, other than the applicant would make a perfect tenant? The best personal reference is a co-signer (see Chapter 2). This is a big step up from words; the referral is backing up their reference with a personal financial guarantee.

You are looking for objective people to find out whether or not an applicant is a good risk to occupy your apartment. A personal reference is only going to give you good information. I doubt if any personal reference is going to tell you the applicant likes to listen to music at the top volume while she gets dressed every morning.

This includes personal references from a parent, uncle, aunt, etc. who are looking out for the best interest of the applicant, not you as the owner or manager. Especially if the personal reference is coming from a person who is currently living with the applicant, you should be aware. Is this person trying to get her friend, who has overstayed her welcome, out of her apartment?

My advice is to accept personal references with a grain of salt.

School Attendance Check

This is serious application checking here. Why do we care if a son or daughter of a rental applicant is in school? Well, if not in school or working, what are they doing all day? What does it matter to you? A sixteen year old not in school at home all day, can eventually get into trouble.

There may be excessive traffic from friends visiting every day.

The parent cannot say what is going on while he or she is at work. Also, a seventeen year old, not working or in school could indicate the parent really does not have control over the child. Get a letter from the school where the child(ren) is suppose to be in attendance on school letterhead stating the full time status of the student.

The Section 8 Verification

One of my applicants indicated verbally that she had a three-bedroom Section 8 certificate for herself and two sons of very different ages. I took her at her word, to my peril. When it came time to sign the lease and other paperwork, the Section 8 department had determined that she was only eligible for a two-bedroom apartment.

Here we were, both owners and the tenant at the lease signing stage, and already in a compromising position. Our mouths were watering to get the apartment rented, so we acquiesced to a two-bedroom rent. That was another example of a mistake I have made in the name of haste and oversight.

Get a copy of the rental applicant's certificate or voucher as part of the pre-screening process. Know up front how many bedrooms the certificate or voucher will cover.

One question that comes up in marketing and leasing classes I have taught are the maximum rent guidelines for Section 8 tenants. Each certificate holder is given the maximum amount of rent the federal or state government will pay for an apartment. This amount changes every year. If you want more rent than what is stated on the Section 8 certificate, you cannot ask the rental applicant to pay the difference as a side deal. With a voucher, you can negotiate with the applicant to pay the extra rent above the voucher amount.

In some states like Rhode Island, you may be able to apply for a special waiver if you can prove that rents in your area are higher than the Section 8 certificate allows. With a Section 8 voucher, if you need to evict for non-payment of rent, you can only claim the amount on the lease, not the side deal amount. For example, the three-bedroom apartment you rented to the Section 8 voucher tenant is $1,700 per month. The certificate was paying for an apartment rent of $1,500 with the tenant paying his or her 30% of income, or $250. You can only sue for $1,500 per month, and not the $1700 you were charging. The lease between you and the Section 8 voucher agency says the rent is $1,500 per month.

Verification Problems

Here are some excuses or reasons an applicant may give you to explain why you cannot verify all of their information. Keep your goal in mind. Don't let their personal issues prevent you from verifying application information. If the applicant has too many roadblocks to your process, move on to the next application.

"I don't know the name of my landlord, or where he lives"

Does this make sense to you? How does the applicant pay the rent? Look at how long the person has lived in the apartment. Ask more questions, like, how did you meet the landlord? What happens if there is an emergency? Tell the person you cannot process the application without complete information. Put it in your "inactive" file until the landlord information is obtained.

"My landlord lives in… (A country outside of the U.S.)"

"That's okay. I am sure they get mail there. Just give me the address."

"I'm living with my girlfriend, and I pay her the rent"

What happened with her own apartment? Why is she living with her girlfriend? For how long? How does she pay, by cash, check or money order? Why aren't both of them on the lease? Does the owner or manager know she is staying there? These are questions to which you need answers.

"I live with my mother"

That's okay, unless the person is thirty-five years old, and never had his or her own apartment. Then the question is, why is an adult with a good job still living with his or her mother? How long has the applicant lived with the mother? Are they both on the lease? Don't assume that the applicant has never left home. Find out how many times the applicant has had to return home to mother.

Perhaps the applicant can't keep an apartment for reasons he or she would rather not disclose. It could be as innocent as a recent divorce or break up, college graduation, relocation, or the loss of a job. It could also be a recent eviction, or a restraining order by the former companion. Make additional inquiries. It could be as innocent as the two of them preferring each other's company. Find out.

"I am an Emancipated Minor"

An emancipated minor is a person, usually under the age of 18 years, who has been granted legal status under the state court system. This means that although the applicant is under the legal age of consent, he or she has been granted the status of an adult by the court system, and can be contractually and legally obligated for any bills, including rent, he or she makes or signs.

Have the applicant provide you with a copy of their documentation as proof that he or she can sign a lease and be legally bound by one. Keep a copy in the applicant's file folder.

Treat this applicant as an adult, because in the eyes of the law, he or she is one. Process the application the same as anyone else's. In many ways, it is to the applicant's credit that he or she has been able to go through the state court system and prove the ability to conduct business as an adult. Do not allow any prejudices you might have about renting to a teenager cloud your verification of the application.

If you still have some reservations, and everything else about the application is good, you may want to consider renting to this applicant with a co-signer (see Chapter 2).

"I've never had my own apartment"

There are single people who have never had their own apartment. You should ask enough questions to satisfy yourself that the applicant has never had his or her own apartment for reasons that would cause you to hesitate renting to him or her. How old is the applicant? Is he 35 years old? Just out of college? How long has he or she held a job?

111

What is his or her income? Your rent could be out of the market for a person who makes $26,000 and is still paying off student loans. Perhaps the applicant lived in an apartment rent-free in his/her parent's house. This could be a reason why he/she could not afford an apartment.

Are there indications that this is a stable, straightforward, reliable person? Does the applicant appear to be a mature, responsible adult? Did the applicant have a roommate in another apartment, and this will be their first apartment alone?

I have had many positive tenancies as the first landlord of an applicant. Do you care if you will be the tenant's first landlord? Do you care whether or not your tenant has no prior renting history? This could be a positive experience for both of you.

"I get paid under the table, so I don't have three pay stubs"

"Under the Table" is undeclared income. You want someone who is legitimately employed. Still, there are those who work for years without filling out a W-2 form. Should you stick to your application-processing plan? Can this applicant claim job security? How? How long has he or she worked for the same employer? Does he or she get a 1099 form every year instead of taking out taxes? How does the applicant pay income taxes? If the tenant gets laid off from work, could he or she at least collect unemployment?

If there is a way to verify employment and income information from the employer, do so. You will still have to decide whether or not you want to take a chance and rent a three-bedroom apartment to a family depending on an under the table income.

"My landlord doesn't know I'm looking for another apartment"

Why should this be a problem? If you decide to move, you will have to give thirty days notice before you can leave his or her apartment anyway. The current landlord can't put the applicant out just because he or she is looking elsewhere. The landlord may actually anticipate a move if he/she just raised the rent.

"I am not comfortable giving you all of my personal information"

Personal information is given out all the time, in exchange for benefits. When a person applies for a car loan, bank loan, credit card, etc. personal information is taken. Applying for an apartment is the same situation. You need specific information in order to determine whether or not you should risk allowing the person or family to occupy your investment property. Be especially wary if the applicant is uncomfortable answering questions needed to verify their ability to pay the rent.

How should you answer that comment? "That's fine. Still, you cannot be considered for this apartment without a written application. I will put your application in my inactive file".

"If you check my credit, I need to tell you that I have a dispute with my (Visa, MasterCard, American Express, etc.) card"

Not everyone will tell you up front they have a credit problem. Still, these days, who hasn't had a credit problem at some point in his or her life? You should be impressed by the applicant's honesty. Go ahead and get a credit report, and see for yourself. It may be worse than what the applicant has told you. Look to see if the dispute is listed on the report.

<u>Chapter 9</u>

The Applicant Family Interview

Interview the finalists for the apartment. This is the chance for the entire family to show you how well behaved they will be in your apartment. It is also your time to get to know your potential future tenant(s). Finally, it is your time to get a sense of how the family interacts with each other, and how they may behave with you.

How the rental applicant and/or the family behaves before he or she gets the keys to your apartment is essential. There are signs that will tell you if you should go ahead and rent the apartment to a specific person or family, or pass on the applicant(s).

You are looking for a quality tenant. At the same time, you do not want to violate your rental applicant's personal, legal, fair housing, or civil rights in your search. You need to be careful about what you ask, and what you do doing your visit. The key word during this part of the process is 'respect'.

<u>Use Specific Interview Questions</u>

You need to develop specific interview questions to ask every applicant. The reason is so you get the same information from each applicant. You also do not want to stumble and ask an illegal question during the interview. Federal fair housing laws prohibit owners from asking certain questions. Even if you accept an applicant, your tenant can sue you for asking an inappropriate question during the interview.

You want to interview the entire family members who will live in the apartment. You can interview the entire family at your office if you have one, or go to their home. We will review both alternatives, and some outcomes experienced during the interview.

Some Examples:

Example #1. I once conducted a family interview at my office. As I spoke with the parents, their four-year old son climbed to the top of my file cabinet, using the front handles like the rungs of a ladder. I paused several times and looked at the child to see if the parents would say something. Finally, I had to ask the child to please get down from his climb. The parents then proceeded to behave like parents. They did not get an apartment.

Example #2: A family interview took place in our office conference room with a single mother and her thirteen-year old daughter. The mother explained that her daughter was mentally challenged, and would we please keep the interview room door closed while the interview took place. The daughter managed to escape from the room several times during the interview, but merely walked around the office quietly until the mother retrieved her.

We accepted the family because the mother had given us advanced warning of her daughter's medical condition and behavior, and explained why she needed a larger apartment due to the situation. Also, when the teenager left the interview room, she was mannerly and did not cause major disruptions in the office. We believed the family deserved the opportunity of a better living environment, and they worked out very well as tenants.

We have rejected applicants unable to get their teenaged son or daughter to attend the mandatory family interview at the office. A parent without control over a child's presence at a family interview is a high-risk.

Example #3. I once interviewed a family at the home of a potential applicant. The teenaged son was not home. He knew that it was important to be there as part of the application process. Still, he made a decision not to attend the family interview. Even more telling, the single mother was embarrassed that the son was not home. It let me know that she did not have control of her son even when it was important to show family unity and cooperation.

The Home Visit

You may decide as part of your selection process to do a home visit for the final three candidates for your apartment. The Home Visit should be conducted after you have gathered all of their basic information such as credit report, landlord report, income verification, etc. This means that the rental applicant has passed your basic selection criteria and is ready to go to the final stages of the process. There is no reason to do a home visit if you have decided not to accept an application.

The main reason for a home visit is to see the conditions under which the rental applicant currently lives. This is different from doing an inspection of the apartment, or to check for housekeeping habits. Messy housekeeping is *not* a reason to reject an applicant. However, abuse of an apartment is a reason to reject.

It is also the place where you can ask questions that you developed by looking at their application and verification returns. You can get clarity on some issues, such as their credit report, criminal offense information, and such.

If you do home visits, and you have roommates as your final applicants, you need to do a home visit at each of the applicants' current homes. If one of your final applicant's lives in a shelter, you need to call the shelter and ask if home visits are allowed. Shelters for battered women are reluctant to allow strangers to know where they are located. You may have to depend on their landlord reference as to whether or not the applicant treats their residence with respect.

The home visit is your opportunity to repeat your ground rules, and to make sure the family is clear about your expectations. You are not guaranteeing them an apartment at this time. You are there to establish whether or not you think the landlord-tenant relationship could work, and to give both you and the applicant a final chance to ask questions and get answers.

Chapter 10

Choosing Your Tenant

So far, the process of selecting your tenant has been a series of qualifications, verifications, and eliminations. You have confirmed the information provided to you, made a determination about the facts, and have either accepted or rejected an application in accordance with the facts presented to you.

If you are lucky, you could end up with more than one candidate eligible for your vacant apartment. If you have processed at least three rental applications for each vacant apartment you have, you could possibly have three or more qualified applicants at the end of your tenant selection process. How will you choose who will get the unit?

Each application must stand on its own merits. Make your decisions on a case-by-case basis. It is probably easier to remove the high-risk contenders from your overall pool first. After all, this is a business decision, where you intend to take the lowest risk by choosing the best candidate from your pool.

What Makes a High Risk Tenant?

- A person who consistently does not pay other bills besides rent;

- A person dishonest about rent payment history. He or she may state that the rent was always paid on time, when in fact, it was always late according to the lease agreement or the owner or manager of the property;

- There is no evidence the rental applicant tried to make good on delinquent bills or past rent;

- A person who has a history of making late rent payments, despite having a consistent employment history;

- A person with a casual attitude regarding the importance of rent;

- Credibility about statements made is impeached;

- Lack of (credible) evidence documenting positive efforts to work with creditors and/or former landlord(s);

- Reasons or excuses why you cannot verify information on their rental application.

- You get a sense the applicant is not cooperating with you or being reasonable about getting you information needed to complete the application;

- The applicant neglects to inform you about information that would have had an even worse impact on your decision;

- When questioned, the rental applicants has lots of excuses and tries to shift blame away from him or herself;

- Makes statements, which directly conflict with written evidence

How Do The Good Ones Get Away?

Sometimes when I hear an owner say that he or she is having a hard time finding quality rental applicants, I hear other things, too. I hear that perhaps the owner has set up so many impediments to the process, that he or she has frightened away or intimidated good potential renters.

Perhaps you have some personal bias against certain types of people. Maybe you heard one too many horror stories from friends and relatives about what happened when they rented to a specific tenant. Whatever your reasons, you could be chopping off your nose to spite your face by limiting your choices of rental applicants.

Selection Process is Too Rigid

You have decided to process and interview the living daylights out of your applicants. Each of them gets the third degree until a high-powered lamp explodes! You have put them through a wringer so tight, the applicant is now afraid to rent from you.

A good applicant doesn't mind going through a reasonable verification process. The effort is appreciated. He or she knows that everyone else in the building now and in the future has gone through a thorough check and screening process, and that you care about who you put in the building. It gives them a sense of comfort.

At the same time, if you screen them to excess, inching into details of their personal life, their friends, etc. it could scare the applicant away. The question could be whether you will be unnecessarily into their personal business during the tenancy.

Owner is Looking For "The Perfect Tenant"

There is no such person. Let's move on.

Too Many Rules

Look at the Open House flyer on Exhibit 1. Does this ad look like the owner really wants to attract applicants? Or, does it appear that the owner is a control freak, to use the phrase nicely? Someone would have to look pretty close to see the advantages of even looking at the apartment from this flyer. One would have to wonder what other rules the owner hasn't even mentioned are lying in wait at the Open House.

Too Much Rent for What Is Offered

This situation usually occurs if you bought your building with the assumption that you could get a specific amount of rent to help carry the mortgage. There could be a problem if you depend on a certain minimum amount of rent in order to make ends meet. You have to find applicants with the ability and willingness to pay what you need.

You can only go so high with a rent amount before it is higher than what a person is willing to pay. If applicants consistently tell you that they like your apartment, but the rent is too much, you need to re-analyze how much you are charging.

Poor Landlord Attitude

If you make the applicant afraid of you during the rental process, he or she may decide to take a pass having you as their landlord. Landlords that come on too strong could scare away applicants who feel you are trying too hard to rent your apartment. Some examples of behavior that should be toned down:

- ➢ Owner asks the same questions over and over again, trying to 'trip up' the applicant's answers;

- ➢ Asking an applicant to 'make up their mind' after you show the apartment before he or she has a chance to digest what has been seen;

- ➢ Antagonizing or threatening an applicant with losing the apartment when verification information comes in slow;

Give the applicant some breathing room!

No Pets

This policy usually comes from an owner or manager's previous bad experience(s). Especially if the owner lives in the building, and has a dog or a cat, this does not go over well with rental applicants. My advice is to be reasonable. If an applicant once had a pet, at some point he or she will want one again. A flexible position would be to allow some kind of pet you feel you could tolerate. Or, look for applicants who are allergic to pets, and can't have one of their own. Remember, an assistive animal is *not* a pet.

Owner is Unwilling To Allow Reasonable Changes to The Apartment

The owner and his wife probably lived in the apartment or the building before moving on to another house, or before deciding to rent out their vacant unit. They want the apartment to stay the way it is, with all the special things they did to it while they were living there. They will not allow any alterations or changes to what they provided when you move in.

The applicant wants to know if chosen, whether he/she can remove the paneling from the living room and paint the walls. You used to live in that apartment, and are fond of the paneling, so you say 'no'. This is not a rational decision, seeing as how you will probably never live in that apartment again. You are holding out your former living quarters for rental income. Let the applicant have permission to do the work under specific guidelines. Don't lose a paying customer over your sentiments on a portion of the real estate.

Poor Building Upkeep

If it is not apparent by looking at the building, an applicant will ask him/herself what you do with the rent money. If the rent is high according to the market, you may find applicants who expect much more for their money. Remember, you are in competition with other owners also showing their apartments. If the outside of your building looks bad, do not expect an applicant to be excited about seeing the inside. Spend some money on paint and repairs to bring the building up to code.

Deteriorated Neighborhood

Not much you can do about your neighborhood, if it is on the down swing. This will limit the kind and number of applicants willing to rent in a neighborhood they fear. You will mainly get applicants who already live in or are familiar with the neighborhood, and do not have a problem with it.

Insufficient Follow-up During The Selection Process

An applicant with good credit, a good job, and money in his or her hand is not going to wait until you get around to processing their application. In the case where you think you have a really good prospect, time is of the essence. You do not want to lose a possible good tenant because you didn't go out of your way to get their information verified as quickly as possible.

The Owner is Not Ready To Rent Out The Vacancy

This usually happens when an apartment has been empty for so long, the owner gets used to it being vacant. If the building is a two family house, for example, and the owner has been living there alone for over a year, he or she may subconsciously be reluctant to put someone in the building again. Perhaps paying the mortgage is not a big issue as far as needing the rent. The owner may like the sense of living in a single-family house.

An owner needs to practice good faith behavior when putting an apartment out to rent. Make sure you are ready to 'let it go' before you advertise. Otherwise, you will always find something wrong with each applicant, so that you can keep the apartment empty.

You Are Afraid You Will Rent to "The Tenant From Hell"

There, I've said it for the first time in this book. This is The Greatest Fear of a Homeowner. I have deliberately stayed away from that phrase. I figured that if you bought this book, that fear was one of your primary reasons for doing so. I prefer to use the term 'high risk tenant' than to perpetuate the stereotype of a person or family so devastating to a homeowner's property and psyche, that he or she would rather keep an income-producing apartment empty than to assume the risk.

It is the fear of making the wrong decision in choosing a tenant that most concerns both owners and property managers. That is why so many new companies catering to security, background checks, credit and criminal checks have proliferated, especially in the Millennium years.

High Risk Tenants do exist in the thousands, probably millions over the planet. Still, when an owner or management company prepares and performs by a *pre-determined tenant selection process*, it takes the emotion out of the final decision, and allows the homeowner or manager to make an informed decision based on facts.

Selection Versus Discrimination

There is a need to emphasize that there is a difference between selecting a tenant, and discriminating against one. If you chose not to consider an applicant because of a personal intolerance, you are practicing discrimination. The federal government states which categories of people in this country who must specifically be included in your selection process and given equal consideration for an apartment.

A Selection:

- You have decided on the candidate who has been working at his job for three years, has good credit, three positive former landlord reports, and no eviction or criminal history. He will pay 40% of his gross income on an $875 per month rent;

- You bought a new house. You are renting out your first house, where you once lived for a number of years. You chose a single person with good credit who will enjoy taking care of the flowers and shrubs you planted over the years. She stayed at her last apartment for ten years. She will pay 37% of her income for renting your two-bedroom apartment.

- You choose a full time student who works part time because she is currently paying more than what you are asking for rent, and has done so for two years. She also collects a small monthly sum of money from a trust fund. She has little credit to report, was prompt in getting you requested information, and had a good landlord reference. She asked good questions about whether or not the building was quiet, so that she could study, and stated she was happy that there were good locks on the doors. You believe this person is stable enough to rent your studio apartment paying 31% of her income for rent;

- Although you have a No Pets policy, you have selected to rent to a tenant with a Seeing Eye Dog. You understand that a Seeing Eye dog is a service animal, and *not* a pet. You also realize that it is against the law to discriminate against a person with a visual disability. He fit all of your ground rules and criteria for selection, and will pay 30% of his income for rent, using a Section 8 certificate;

Discrimination:

- You have not rented out your empty two-bedroom apartment for three months. You have not liked the kind of people who have applied: single mothers with young children, Section 8 certificate holders, racially mixed singles who want to rent as roommates. You are prepared to hold out as long as possible until the "right" kind of family knocks on your door;

- You have a qualified applicant who will pay 26% of income toward the rent. You will not rent to the couple because they have a child under 6 years of age, and you have a swimming pool in the back yard. Also, even though the apartment has been de-leaded, the common hallways have not. You don't want the potential liability;

- You have a two-bedroom apartment on the first floor, but refuse to consider a blind person or one with a physical disability because you are afraid the person could fall down the front stairs and sue you;

- You will not rent to a woman in a wheelchair who wants to rent your second floor apartment because she will need and has asked to build a wheel chair lift. You do not want to have one on your property, even if the she pays for the work to be done;

- You have an applicant who would pay 28% of his income toward the $875 rent for your two-bedroom. You do not intend to rent him the apartment because his 'kind of people' can't seem to hold down a job, even though he has a work history of five years at the same place of employment

Notice that in Selection, I did not mention any decisions based on race, ethnicity, disability, status as a parent, or source of income. Selections were made according to ability to pay, income and credit history, and other factual information. In the Discrimination Section, decisions are made based on information that has very little to do with ability to pay, landlord references, income, or any eviction histories.

You should not allow an assumption or bias about your applicants prevent you from doing business and being in a position to collect a monthly income. If you do, you are breaking the law. Read Chapter 13 *on Federal Fair Housing Laws* to bring yourself up to the current housing laws of the United States.

Carolyn Gibson

<u>Chapter 11</u>

How to Reject an Applicant

" How do I tell a person I have not selected him or her for the apartment?'

Notify those applicants you have decided to reject as soon as possible. When you receive a completed rental application, you should review the entire document to make sure that the applicant has the basic eligibility requirements for the apartment. Separate those rental applications that do not qualify at all for your apartment. For example, if you have a family of three people apply for a one-bedroom apartment, you should inform them that their family is too large for the unit size. You may have several applications with bad credit reports, poor landlord reports, or could have more family members than you have bedrooms.

You should not wait until you have processed all of your applications before you tell a truly unqualified applicant you have rejected their application. Let the applicant know you have eliminated him or her as a candidate. Give the person the opportunity to look elsewhere for an apartment.

Many landlords find the rejection part of the tenant selection process distasteful. They do not know what to say. They are afraid of what the applicant will say or do. They like the applicant, feel bad about the rejection, and do not know how to express themselves. Here is where having a selection process will let you 'off the hook' so to speak.

131

Put some thought into how you will inform the applicant that he or she has not been selected for the apartment. A rejection is not the same as a non-selection of an applicant. Especially if there is only one apartment available to rent, there can only be one person for the unit.

"The vacancy has been filled. Would you like me to keep your application on file in case there is another vacancy at a later time?"

If the applicant calls you, the conversation should be kept polite but brief. I prefer to use the term 'you have not been selected' rather than to say 'you have been rejected for the apartment'. It sounds less harsh to the applicant, and gives the person some dignity.

"I have selected a tenant for my apartment. I received many applications, and I made a decision to choose another person"

"Your application has been removed from my process due to insufficient income to pay the rent"

The applicant will want to know the reason for the rejection. Some may try to make you reconsider your decision, or even argue over a point regarding your decision. You should have some idea what you will tell the applicant. The main point is that you had a selection and criteria process that was used. The applicant knew up front what aspects of their application were going to be considered. Unfortunately, you only had one apartment available, and several applications from which to choose.

"What if the applicant becomes confrontational?"

You should be prepared for some resistance, questions, and even anger from an applicant. After all, remember everything you put him or her through as a rental applicant. The rental applicant may feel led on about the apartment because of the attention and detail you put into processing the application. If it was not clear to the applicant that the process was not a guarantee of an apartment, the applicant may feel anger, if not frustration, that all of his or her efforts did not result in getting the apartment.

Think of the rejection in the same way as if you have been rejected for a job you really wanted. You want to know what you could have done to better persuade the human resource manager to pick you for the job. Again, here is where your tenant selection process will help you. The answer may be *"I wanted a tenant that would pay no more than 40% of his or her income towards the rent. Your application indicated that you would pay almost 49% of your income towards the rent. This percentage is too high for my comfort level"*.

Note that I do not make any personal statements about the applicant. I do not say or imply that the applicant was not selected because he or she did not make me feel warm and fuzzy. I attempt to make comments based on concrete information and facts. Certainly, if you and the applicant have not been "connecting" during the tenant selection process, and you felt uncomfortable considering him or her as a tenant, you have the right to reject the person on that basis. See Chapter 7 on "Signs There May Be a Problem".

You should be able to tell the tenant that during the process, you felt that if there were a problem between you regarding rent payment, repairs, complaints, etc. that the two of you would not be able to discuss the matter openly and freely. You need to rent to a person with whom you think you can work, and you do not get that impression with him or her.

No one likes to feel or believe that he or she is not qualified, whether for a job, an apartment, or admission to a private school. You should expect the applicant to ask specific questions to which perhaps you cannot give an answer. Present or previous landlords may have given you information that caused you to reject an applicant. The landlord may have confirmed what your instincts have been telling you about what a tenancy would be like with the applicant. That information was given to you in confidence. You cannot then turn around and tell the applicant what a landlord said to get you off the hook.

You could say, *"One of the confidential landlord references did not indicate to me that you would be a successful candidate for my apartment. I am a very strict owner, and although you would probably be fine renting from a different owner, the references I received, plus the number of applications I had to choose from caused me to choose another person".*

Credit bureaus are very strict about owners giving out an applicant's credit information. If you rejected an applicant based on his or her credit report, say so, and give the applicant the information to go to the credit bureau in question for specific details.

Let the applicant know that you realize that he/she is disappointed, but state firmly that *your decision has been made and is final.* If it is true, you can let the person know he or she was one of your top three applicants. You will keep their application on file for a year. At the same time, do not give them renewed or false hope.

Naturally, if the rejection is one that will remain a rejection regardless of time, you need to let the person know that there were some areas in which he or she did not fit into your selection process, such as insufficient income or savings. You might say that your selected applicant had a longer renting history, or that he or she had held their job for a longer period of time. This way, you are giving the rejected applicant some sense of how he or she can present a better application or address the issues you raised to another homeowner.

Whatever you do, don't lie to get yourself off the hook. Applicants can sense dishonesty and insincerity, and it will come back to hurt you. Be as fair and honest about your decision as possible. After all, your job was to select the most qualified applicant that will ensure you that the rent will be paid on time each month, with as little maintenance, disturbance or other problems possible.

Remember, if you have to reject an applicant, you should still have at least two other applications in active processing mode. You should not be in a position where you are afraid that if you reject a high-risk applicant, you will lose time and money if you move on to another application.

Naturally, if your decision to reject a person is based on some form of discrimination against the person (for example, the children were all under 6 years of age, which is familial status discrimination), you should expect more vehement questioning by the applicant. Perhaps he or she has encountered similar rejections, even with an outstanding application. He or she may try to solicit you to see if the

135

children were an issue, or the fact that the applicant has a different religion than yourself. Do not expect any sympathy if the applicant decides to take his or her case to the state commission of discrimination, or the federal fair housing bureau in your state.

You should keep the rental application of all persons you rejected for at least three years in a file folder for your records.

HUD Handbook 4350.3 on Rejecting an Applicant[19]

[They are] ineligible, as defined in paragraph 2-16a if,

They do not meet the owner's tenant selection criteria;

They are unable to disclose and document all Social Security numbers or execute a certification when numbers have not been assigned;

They failed to sign and submit verification consents......and relevant individual verification consents. However, [there may be reasons] ...concerning permissible delays in signing these consents due to extenuating circumstances.

---

[19] Go to http://www.hudclips.gov for complete synopsis

<u>Chapter 12</u>

What to Do After the Applicant is Accepted

Y ou have made your decision. You now have the tenant or family you have decided is the best one to rent your apartment. This is not the time to weaken to suggestions to change your policies, or to allow yourself to compromise your process. It is not yet finished.

<u>Avoid Side Deals</u>

You can turn a perfectly good tenant into a potential problem by allowing a side deal. Any side deal about the condition of the apartment, the rent, when it is to be paid, etc. is best not to happen. Again, all of your decisions about how the apartment will be treated or any special arrangements agreed to, should have been decided before you started to take applications.

We discussed this situation in Chapter 2. Still, it is worth visiting again, because the subject may come up again after you have accepted the applicant. It usually comes up if the building is in disrepair. The applicant may figure you are willing to make a deal.

You may have the tenant approach you with a 'dilemma'. He or she has been laid off from work, and asks to take care of the entire property in exchange for free rent on a temporary basis. Now we have privacy and favoritism issues with the other residents, loss of rent, control of emergency work, and other concerns.

Let us continue. Let's say the applicant offers to do maintenance work or cleaning on the property in lieu of rent, or for part of the rent. You have no idea what the potential tenant's work is like, or what his or her work habits are like. How do you know he or she is reliable enough to do the work? How will you control what to do if the tenant fails to do the work?

Let's say the rent is $800 per month, with $100 a month taken off for cleaning the property. You will need to put together a list of responsibilities at the property. Both parties have to agree *in writing* that the work outlined is worth $100 per month. You don't want the tenant coming to you later, saying that he or she thinks $100 is too little an amount for what you are asking to be done at the property.

There you will have a problem. If the tenant decides he or she doesn't want to do the work any more, you will have to do it yourself again, or hire a company to get the work done. If the parting of the ways regarding this arrangement does not go well, you could have a problem collecting the $100 as part of the total rent of $800 per month. The tenant may decide to continue to withhold that amount as compensation for time he or she thought should have been paid to him or her. You would then have to take the person to small claims court, or housing court for unpaid rent.

If you insist on doing it, a side deal is worthless unless it is in writing. There lies another potential problem. Should the lease say the rent is $800 per month, or $700 per month? If it says $700 per month, and the arrangement doesn't work out, how will you collect the $100? You will need an attorney to help work this entire matter out in the lease.

You will need to keep your rent and building expenses separate. There needs to be an understanding about what the tenant can spend, where to get supplies, and how much supplies are needed. You could get into an argument about what is a major or minor repair, what the expenses were and what they cost. How will you determine how much snow removal or landscaping is worth the time and efforts of your tenant? Will the tenant shovel the sidewalk and keep the paths as clean as you desire? Will the grass get cut on a regular basis, and weeds removed? If not, and another tenant slips and falls on ice or wet grass, you will have to cover that accident through your insurance company.

After all of this, you may finally decide it is better to keep just one relationship with the tenant.

"I really like the apartment, but the rent is too much. Would you consider lowering it by $50?"

"No, I won't". He knew what the rent was when he applied for the unit. Moreover, he probably thinks that you may be willing to lower the rent rather than to start the application process all over again, and lose rent in the meantime.

This is **your** property, which means you get to call the shots. Do not fold to intimidation or out of financial desperation. If you begin by letting a tenant decide how much rent he or she will pay, you have already lost control of the apartment.

Tell the person that the rent is firm, and that you hope he will still take the apartment at the agreed rent amount. Besides, if he decides not to take the apartment, you should still have two other applications in process mode you can contact. I say 'should' because many owners and managers will stop processing applications when they think they have a good candidate in hand. You never know you have a tenant until the paperwork (lease, move-in inspection, security deposit receipt, etc.) is signed, the money is in your hand, and keys have been turned over.

"Can I lower the rent by cleaning the building?"

This should have been addressed at the beginning of the process. It needs to be a decision you made well in advance of choosing a tenant. If you agree to do this, you are changing the nature of the relationship. The tenant becomes not just your tenant, but your employee as well. You need to keep the two relationships separate if possible.

Get a Security Deposit

A security deposit is not rent. It is money set aside to pay for unpaid rent and/or damages to the apartment. Whether or not security deposit money will be withheld is assessed once the tenant moves out. It is *not* 'extra' income for the owner.

Security deposit money is supposed to be kept, in most states, in an interest bearing bank account separate and apart from your personal or business funds. You are also required to give the tenant a receipt for the amount of the funds, with information on which bank the deposit is held. A copy of the receipt should go to the tenant, and a copy in your tenant file folder.

In some states, such as Massachusetts, if you take a security deposit and last month's rent, you must put all of this money in the tenant's interest bearing account and pay an annual interest. Recent laws have changed from state to state geared toward protecting tenant's escrowed funds. It is your duty to check with your local real estate board or state house for a copy of your state's current security deposit law.

The security deposit should be paid before the tenant is allowed to move into your apartment. My advice is to get the security deposit in the form of a certified check or money order. That way, you know the funds are good. If you take cash (which I never advise), then you are responsible for giving the tenant a written receipt for the cash, with a copy for your tenant and income tax files.

The security deposit should be accepted with the thought that, all things considered, such as the amount of time the tenant lived in the apartment, the condition of the apartment when he or she moved in, etc., it will be refunded to the tenant minus unpaid rent and any damages. Wear and tear situations are not deductible from the security deposit. Damages, vandalism, leaving furniture in the apartment and such can be deducted. You will have to list what you are deducting, why, and the amount you are not giving back.

If you performed an Apartment Inspection form when you moved in the tenant, then take this out of the file folder. Go through it with the tenant and compare the condition of the unit at move-in with the condition at move-out.

"I'm waiting for my landlord to return my security deposit"
"My Mother is Going to Pay the Security Deposit"

This is the applicant's personal problem, and has nothing to do with you. This matter should have been established at the beginning of the rental process. One should never count on funds that the applicant does not have in hand. What if the applicant doesn't get the security deposit back? It is poor financial planning on the part of the applicant. He or she is depending on a source of income that is not based on savings, anticipating moving from one apartment to another. This may be an indication that the applicant lives on the edge every month.

You should have confirmed the fact that the applicant had the funds in hand at the beginning of the selection process. If you did not check the applicant's eligibility, and he or she does not have the security deposit, you really need to move on to the next applicant.

"May I Pay the Security Deposit Over Time?"

"No, you may not", or "No, that is not acceptable" are some of the correct answers. You verified through the selection process that the rental applicant had the income and the necessary funds to complete the tenancy transaction. If the applicant does not have all of the money available to rent your apartment upon acceptance, then move on to another person who has their money *in hand*.

The record-keeping nightmare caused by taking a security deposit on a payment plan is horrific. Get it all up front.

Get the First Month's Rent

The applicant should not only have the first month's rent and security deposit in hand and readily available, but there should be more than those funds in the bank. If the applicant gives you everything he or she has in the bank, how will the second month's rent be paid? If you are asked to wait for the first and last month's rent and security deposit once the applicant is accepted, your applicant's real ability to pay is in serious doubt.

You need to get a guaranteed form of the first month's rent and security deposit. In spite of everything you have done to pick the best tenant, things can still go wrong until the key is turned over. Ask that the first month's rent and security deposit be paid separately by money order or certified check. This way, the security deposit can go directly into the tenant's escrow savings account, and the rent in the building operating fund account. These are assured funds that let you know that you and the tenant have started off on the right foot.

I never recommend accepting cash. So many things can go wrong. It also sets up a bad precedent between you and the tenant. You and the tenant want and need to have proof that funds are paid each month. If you *insist* on taking cash, make sure you immediately give the tenant a receipt. Keep a second copy of the receipt in the tenant's file folder.

Do not sign a lease until you have the applicant's money **in your hand**. The same goes for the keys to the apartment. If you do not give out a lease and have a month-to-month tenancy, do not give out keys until you have been paid.

Renter's Insurance

I strongly recommend that during the lease signing period, you tell the tenant about Renter's Insurance. This is available for non-homeowners to cover any damages and losses while living in the apartment due to fire, flood, theft, etc. The amount of the insurance is very economical, and is based on the amount of coverage wanted by the tenant. Many owners are now including a clause in their lease that states renter's insurance is either recommended or required by the tenant. You should have something in writing stating that the tenant was told about renter's insurance, signed and dated by the tenant, to put in his or her file folder.

"I'm waiting for my student loan to come through"

How many times will you hear that phrase in the future, after he or she moves in? When is it expected? How many months' rent will it cover? What if the student is not approved? Did you verify they had enough money to pay the rent when you first took the rental application? Did you verify the source of the applicant's income? Why not?

You should have received an award letter from the college stating the nature of the student's financial package, whether a loan, scholarship, grant, etc. the amount of the total package, whether or not it can be used for housing, and when the funds will be issued.

"A local charity is going to pay the first month's rent"

Wait a minute. The applicant was supposed to show proof of income *in advance* of being accepted for the apartment. What happened to the money? Was this ever mentioned at the interview? Owners, managers, and real estate brokers should confirm or verify that the rental applicant actually has the rent and security deposit early in the process, not a month before they are suppose to move in.

Pin Down the Move-In Date

This is where the rubber meets the road, or in some cases, falls off the tire. You ask when he or she can move into the apartment, and you are sometimes answered with excuses.

"I have to give my current landlord thirty days notice"

Most times this situation cannot be helped. This is why you should notify the applicant that you have accepted him or her as quickly as possible. You wouldn't want your tenant to move out without giving you advance notice. Respect the applicant for giving his or her current landlord the same courtesy.

Just to make sure you have a deal, you may want to ask the applicant for some good faith money on the security deposit. If you have to move to another applicant for some reason, then by receiving funds as a security deposit, you have not established tenancy.

"I just lost my job, but I'm starting another one next week."

Losing a job is different from being laid off from a job. First make sure which situation is under discussion. Second, the applicant should have notified you of his or her change of income status as soon as it was implemented. Third, if the applicant tells you that he or she just switched jobs, I would question why they would not have told you about those plans earlier. The applicant must have known h/she was looking for a new job when the rental application was completed. Fourth, why would an applicant not wait until h/she secured the new apartment before taking on a new job? This would raise concerns for me as an owner.

When you made your decision to approve a specific applicant, you did so thinking that you had a gainfully employed person or family. You no longer have one. Something went astray, but whatever it was cannot be made your problem. There is no guarantee that the new job will be as successful as the one the applicant just left, unless he or

145

she has an employment contract. Also, the employment income and history with the employer is now gone.

This is a state of affairs where you will have to make a judgment call. One good way to gauge your decision whether or not to go ahead and rent the apartment is the income savings. You know from the bank income verification whether or not the applicant has enough money to cover the rent for more than one month, and the security deposit. You can make a judgment call as to whether or not you think or trust the applicant will keep the new job, and will be able to pay the rent without a problem in the future, especially if the person or family has a good sized bank account.

If you want to take a chance based upon the applicant's average employment history, savings, good credit history, etc. do so. Understand you have decided to shift from your process, that is your prerogative and right as the owner.

Section 8 Tenants

You cannot schedule a move-in date until you have an approved apartment and building inspection in hand, a Housing Assistance Payments (HAP) Contract with the Section 8 agency, a signed lease and Lead Paint Disclosure form from the Section 8 agency, and the first month's rent and full security deposit in hand from the tenant. The Section 8 agency will forward their portion of the first month's rent once you sign and return the lease and HAP Contract.

If you move in a Section 8 certificate or voucher holder before all the approvals and paperwork has been completed, signed and accepted, you do so at your peril. You will not receive any subsidy payments retroactive to the actual move-in date, only the date the paperwork and approvals were received and accepted by the housing agency. The tenant is responsible for paying his/her share of the first month's rent and the entire security deposit.

The Apartment Inspection

This is where you could lose your potential tenant if you have not done some basic marketing work on your own behalf. Make sure that the apartment has been sufficiently repaired and cleaned before you give out the key. Check to see if all the windows move up and down with ease. Are all the window screens installed? Flush the toilet and look in the kitchen and medicine cabinets. Potential tenants will back out of a deal and not sign a lease if the apartment looks essentially the same way it did when you first showed it to them, especially if you showed it in the process of being fixed up.

You need to be sure the tenant is satisfied with the apartment *in writing* at the time of the move-in. The Apartment Inspection Form[20], a Video, or Pictures is the best way to prove the condition of the apartment before the family moved in, and that the tenant moved in satisfied with the conditions as presented.

The condition of the apartment before the tenant moved in is very important to document. This is the basis upon which the security deposit will or will not be refunded when the tenant moves out. Also, when or if a landlord-tenant relationship ever goes bad, the condition of the apartment upon move-in is many times the first thing a tenant will mention.

---

[20] Exhibit 5

Have two copies of the inspection form prepared. Do the inspection either before or *preferably*, with the new tenant. If there are any repair, replacement or cleanliness discrepancies, they should be recorded on the apartment inspection sheet at the time of the inspection. If you videotape or use a camera, those items will speak for themselves.

All parties to the lease must sign both copies of the move-in inspection. Give one to the tenant, and keep one for your files. Your tenant may ask for a copy of the videotape or pictures you took; make and give a copy to him or her at your expense. You have nothing to hide, right?

Tell the tenant to report any items not recorded from the apartment move-in inspection to you in writing within ten days after the tenant has moved in. Give him or her your telephone number or address where he or she can contact you. A handle could fall off a kitchen cabinet, or a window could stick after a hot day.

Some states, and all Section 8 certificate and voucher holders, require that the city or subsidized housing inspectors inspect and approve the apartment before you can move in a tenant. Usually there is a fee involved. If the apartment is acceptable, the city will issue you a certificate of inspection, stating that the unit was up to code before the tenant moved in. This will be especially handy in the event there is a dispute regarding the security deposit.

Keep A Waiting List

You have successfully selected a tenant, moved the person or family into the unit, and you take a sigh of relief. You have chosen the person or family that you want to occupy your vacant apartment. What is next? What do you do with all those rental applications you have collected?

A 'waiting list' is what is called of all the eligible and qualified applications you processed, but did not complete. You never know what will happen with your top contender. She could have a family emergency, and have to leave town permanently. Perhaps he was laid off from work unexpectedly, and doesn't know when he will find another job.

Keep the top two applicants you also processed along with the one you selected to move into your apartment in your file cabinet. In case the tenant you selected doesn't work out, finds a better apartment, changes his or her mind, etc., you will already have two or more applications fully processed.

Notify everyone as soon as possible that you have made a selection, by telephone or mail. Otherwise, your applicants will keep calling to find out their status. Also, you want the applicants to be able to accept another apartment he or she applied for elsewhere, if you have not chosen him or her. This is the fair thing to do. Besides, if your top three candidates do not work out or have found another apartment, you will want the goodwill of the remaining applicants on your list.

Sometimes, if you have had a number of apartments to fill, an applicant will ask if you are keeping a waiting list. He or she will want to know where they stand. What order will you keep the applications? How will you know who will be first, second, or third in line for the next vacancy?

File all the applications you collected for your building in your file cabinet for future reference. Do not throw them away. Make a file folder for the top two candidates who weren't chosen, the rejected ones, and your acceptable applications. It is a good idea to indicate the date and time the applicant is placed on the waiting list. You need to be prepared in the event a rejected applicant sues you for discrimination. You should keep your rental applications and other paperwork for at least six months.

Chapter 13

Federal Housing Laws

How and why does the federal government have anything to do with your tenant selection process? First and foremost, the United States Constitution declared on July 4, 1776 "that all men are created equal...with certain unalienable rights....". Since 1866, the United States Congress has established a series of laws designed to ensure that every adult person, male or female, has the same or equal opportunity to rent an apartment as the next person. The inclusion of the United States Fair Housing Laws are designed to ensure that the opportunity to rent an apartment or home of choice is guaranteed as a part of the Declaration of Independence's "pursuit of happiness" entitlement to mankind.

State and federal fair housing laws are designed to help owners avoid discriminatory behavior that results in a rental applicant's belief that he or she has been treated unfairly. According to federal law, when you select a tenant for your vacant apartment, every interested person is supposed to have an equal chance at renting your apartment. An owner does not have an absolute right to reject a rental applicant based upon the applicant's religious or ethnic background, sex, marital status, or physical and mental condition.

This chapter is designed to give you a brief overview of the federal fair housing acts and their intents. I am not an attorney, and this section does not attempt to give you legal advice. Consider this information as notice that although you own your home or investment property, your property

151

is under the jurisdiction of United States Federal and State Laws as provided in the Constitution. Many owners get into trouble because they fail to observe or acknowledge this fact.

The Civil Rights Act of 1866

This Act followed the Constitution's 13th Amendment enacted in 1865, which formally abolished slavery. It guarantees all citizens equal rights under the law to inherit, purchase, lease, sell, hold, and convey real and personal property.

The Civil Rights Act of 1964

This federal law prohibits discrimination in public accommodations, including federally assisted programs, and in employment on the basis of race, color, religion, sex, or national origin. This means that if you accept a Section 8 certificate or voucher, you must accept, process, and consider that applicant's rental application equally, along with all your other applications.

The Civil Rights, or Fair Housing Act of 1968, Title VIII

Under Section 804 of this Act, it is unlawful to:

Refuse to rent to a person after he or she has made a bona fide offer; or to refuse to negotiate for the rental of a vacancy or otherwise make unavailable or deny an apartment or dwelling (such as a single family house) because of the person's race, color, religion, sex, familial status, handicap, or national origin;

Refusal to make reasonable accommodations in rules, policies, practices, or services, when such accommodations may be necessary to afford such person equal opportunity to use and enjoy a dwelling or apartment.

The 1988 Fair Housing / Civil Rights Act Amendment

This fair housing act added the following rental applicants as protected against discrimination practices: physically and mentally disabled or handicapped, and families with children under 18 years of age. This means that you cannot refuse to rent your apartment to a family with children under the age of 18 years. It also means that you cannot refuse to rent an apartment to a pregnant woman, or a person or persons in the process of adopting children.

This is an important Act, as monetary awards can be for actual damages as well as for non-economic injuries such as embarrassment, humiliation, inconvenience, and mental anguish.

HUD Policy Subsection 5. Owner Policies (Fair Housing Act and Section 504 of The Rehabilitation Act)[21]

2-47. NON-DISCRIMINATION regarding services, policies and practices:

a. Owners may not provide services or follow policies or practices that discriminate, on the basis of handicap, against a qualified individual with handicaps. (Section 504 and Fair Housing Act)

---

[21] HUD Handbook 4350.3 CHG-24, page 2-76, 1/93

EXAMPLES: Prohibiting an individual with handicaps to use an assistive device, asking different questions of individuals with handicaps and individuals without handicaps in the application interview.

b. Owners shall not fail to provide reasonable accommodations when such accommodations may be necessary to afford a handicapped person equal opportunity to use and enjoy a unit and the public and common areas. (Fair Housing Act)

EXAMPLES: Put up signs to assist persons who have handicaps, allow mail-in procedures, relocate services to accessible locations, keep passageways clear of obstructions, ask same questions of all applicants.

c. Owners shall provide adjustments to policies and practices that do not discriminate, on the basis of handicap, against a qualified individual with handicaps. (Section 504 of the Rehabilitation Act)

EXAMPLES: Permit assistive devices, auxiliary alarms, assistive animals.

The Rehabilitation Act of 1973

This federal law prohibits discrimination against persons with disabilities in all federally assisted and low income tax credit housing programs.

Owners and managers frequently ask the question of what constitutes a disability. For example, a person can be considered disabled if he or she is addicted to drugs or alcohol. At the same time, it is **not** discrimination to reject such an applicant if it can be proved that the applicant is actively indulging in drugs or alcohol, or has been convicted of selling illegal substances.

Under this law, if a disabled tenant requests an assigned parking space if you are renting a building with a parking lot, you must comply with that request. If a tenant asks for a bathroom grab bar for the toilet and/or bathtub use, or needs a wheelchair ramp because he or she is no longer able to maneuver stairs to get into the building, you must grant that request.

Some states mandate that the owner pay for these modifications and/or adjustments; others require that the tenant needing the service must pay for it. It is highly recommended that you research your state laws regarding complying with a disabled tenant's request for these and other services.

American with Disabilities Act of 1990

Mandates that places of public accommodation, such as parking lots, community rooms, leasing and management offices, must be accessible to people with mobility, visual, and hearing impairments, regardless of the age of the property.

U.S. Department of Housing and Urban Development: Tenant Modifications of Premises (Fair Housing Act)[22].

a. A person with handicaps has the right under the Fair Housing Act to make reasonable modifications to any part of his or her unit or the common areas at his or her own expense.

---

[22] HUD Handbook 4350.3 change 24, page 2-62, 1/93

1) The owner must permit the modifications if they are reasonable and may be necessary to afford a handicapped person full enjoyment of the premises.

2) The owner may, where it is reasonable to do so, condition permission for a modification on the renter's agreeing that when s/he vacates the unit s/he will restore the interior of the premises to the condition that existed before the modification, reasonable wear and tear excepted.

EXAMPLE: For marketing reasons or operational considerations, the owner may require the tenant to raise cabinets that have been lowered or replace roll-under lavatories with the previously existing vanity/sink combination.

3) The owner may not increase for persons with handicaps any required security deposit. However, where it is necessary in order to ensure with reasonable certainty that funds will be available to pay for restorations at the end of the tenancy, the owner may negotiate as part of such a restoration agreement a provision requiring that the tenant pay into an interest bearing escrow account, over a reasonable period, a reasonable amount of money not to exceed the cost of the restorations. The interest of such an account shall accrue to the benefit of the tenant.

4) The owner may condition permission for a modification on the renter providing reasonable assurances that the work will be done in a workmanlike manner and that any required building permits will be obtained.

Lead Paint Disclosure Act

In 1978, lead based paint was banned nationwide for consumer use. As a homeowner renting out your apartment, you are required by HUD Title 24 CFR, Part 35 Subtitle A, to disclose to the lessee the presence of any known lead-based paint and/or hazards; provide available records and reports; provide the lessee and any subleases with a lead paint hazard information pamphlet.[23] If you have a lead paint certificate indicating that the building and apartment has been freed of lead paint and inspected by a state certified inspector, a copy of this certificate may be provided in place of a disclosure document.[24]

Service Animals[25]

Service animals that assist persons with disabilities are considered to be auxiliary aids and are exempt from the pet policy and from the refundable pet deposit. Examples include guide dogs for persons with vision impairments, hearing dogs for persons with hearing impairments, and emotional assistance animals for persons with chronic mental illness.

Civil Rights Acts Enforcement Measures

A person who believes a landlord or housing manager is discriminating against him or her may sue in the Federal Court. The court has the right to order the owner or property manager to rent to the plaintiff if the judge believes discrimination has taken place. In addition, the court may award monetary damages to the rental applicant.

---

[23] http://www.hud.gov

[24] 24 CFR Subtitle A 35.80 and 35.82

[25] U.S. Department of HUD definition

Carolyn Gibson

Chapter 14

Expectations and Guarantees

Throughout this book, I have given you the benefits of my personal and professional successes and failures as a residential property manager. What I have learned is that no matter how well or extensive you process a rental application, there will always be factors beyond your control. No one can guarantee a 100% perfect tenant every time a selection is made. Property managers and/or owners with years of experience selecting tenants can never be absolutely certain if their selection will be a good or bad one.

Owning a home is a financial risk. So is renting out an apartment. You should not be afraid to rent out your apartment, no more than you were afraid to buy a house. You minimize your risks by making carefully planned decisions, and acting on them.

There will always be the exception to the rule in picking an applicant for a vacant apartment. What is important is that you have a method or use standards by which you can determine the best probability of a successful rental. Read those chapters of this book where you think you need more information, or those chapters regarding fair housing, so that you minimize any liability from illegal activities.

There is never a guarantee that anyone can select the "perfect" tenant. I have selected many good families, most with a single mother with good children. I rented a unit to one such applicant. For years, the rent was paid on time, the apartment was well maintained, and I had no problems. Suddenly one year, the rent started to come in late each month, complaints started to come in from other tenants, and when I went to inspect the apartment, it was a mess.

Turned out that once the children became teenagers, negative peer pressure entered the picture. Invariably, one teenager succumbed to drugs, or a gang, or whatever else had a negative impact on the family. The parent worked hard to keep and maintain control. Still, a person can only do so much, and eventually I had to evict the family.

The point is that one can only expect to select the best candidate out of the several rental applicants you have at your disposal at the time. Once your selection is made, the only guarantee you have is the first and last month's rent, and the security deposit in hand. After that, it is up to the facts you obtained, and the relationship you and your applicant established during the selection process.

<u>Summary</u>

After reading this book, you may ask, how does anyone ever get their vacant apartment rented with so many things to look out for with an applicant? It may seem that you have an awful lot of things to check, do, and observe. Even if you do everything right, you could still end up with a problem tenant.

The point of this book is to show you what techniques are available to use when renting out your investment property. Here are some final points to remember:

> ➢ It is easier and cheaper to reject a rental applicant, than to evict a person or family after they have moved into your property;

> ➢ It takes approximately four weeks to process a rental application. In some states, it could take twelve weeks to evict a family for cause other than non-payment of rent. Spend the time up front to check out your rental applicants;

> ➢ Don't be in a hurry to put someone into your vacant apartment. Take the time to rent to the right person, not just the most convenient one;

> ➢ Even if you think you have the Rental Applicant of the Year, continue to process the other applications. Something can always go wrong at the last minute, and you do not want to take this applicant just because you failed to follow through with the other applications. Cover yourself at all times;

➤ Use your best judgment when reviewing a person's rental application. Not every piece of questionable information means that the applicant is a bad risk. Look at the overall picture;

➤ Invest in registering with a credit bureau who can verify the tenant's payment history;

➤ Check out friends and relatives as if they are strangers. They could have problems about which you are not aware that could pose a potential problem for you later;

➤ Renting your apartment should not be done like it is an emergency. It is a *process* best done thoroughly;

➤ Do not let anyone rush you into renting them an apartment. Never be so desperate to start getting rent on your apartment that you overlook the obvious or skip steps in processing the rental application;

➤ Renting your apartment should be conducted in a professional, business like manner;

➤ It is your responsibility to ensure that your house is in legal compliance with the law, state building codes, health and safety codes, etc. Pay now to make sure your house is in order, or pay later if/when something goes wrong;

➤ Ignorance of The Law is No Excuse. If you rent apartments in exchange for money, you are conducting a business. There are federal, state and city laws that govern how and to whom you can rent out your apartment. Take the time to research the laws in your state regarding fair housing to avoid litigation that could take years and plenty of legal bills, not to mention money, to resolve;

➢ There are no guarantees in renting out an apartment. People change, and their circumstances can change. If you know you did everything you could to fairly and accurately process a rental application, you will be rewarded in most cases with a good tenant.

➢ I cannot say it enough: *invest in hiring a good real estate attorney*. A lawyer is not a person hired just to show up for a closing. He or she is your legal information resource to ensure that your rights and property are protected. Whatever you pay your attorney will be worth it if the information prevents you from being fined, lose an eviction case, jeopardize your insurance policy, being sued by your tenant(s), and any other possible disaster that can happen to a homeowner.

Carolyn Gibson

Web Site Information

This listing was developed to provide additional information regarding property management, tenant screening and selection. For legal advice, always consult your attorney.

Most local libraries have a computer or two available for those who need to look something up on the Internet.

Excellent web sites for small homeowners and landlords
http://www.mrlandlord.com

http://www.landlord.com

Institute of Real Estate Management (IREM)
http://www.irem.org

National Association of Realtors (NAR)
http://www.realtor.com

National Apartment Association (NAA)
For owners of multi-family apartment buildings
http://www.naahq.org

Good Site for Getting Legal Information on Tenant Screening
http://www.nolo.com

U.S. Department of Housing & Urban Development
Official Federal Government Web Site (H.U.D.)
http://www.hud.gov

Information on Service Animals in Housing
http://www.deltasociety.org

Web site that provides national real estate information
http://www.homefair.com

Property management computer software
http://www.tenantpro.com

A good explanation of the Beacon Score for
Checking Credit Rating
http://www.oskie.com/credit-bureau-tips.htm

Listing of national security deposit laws
http://www.rentlaw.com/securitydeposit.htm

Exhibit 1

Sample Apartment for Rent Sign

APARTMENT FOR RENT

Two Bedroom Apartment in a three family house on the second floor.
Owner occupies the first floor apartment.
Last tenant stayed ten years. Apartment has been remodeled and updated.

Large bedrooms, living room with ceiling fan, carpet, eat-in kitchen, and two room air conditioners.
Gas Heat and Hot Water, Electric Stove. Tenant pays own utility bills.
No Pets Allowed.
Street Parking Only.
Prefer No Home Businesses.
Cable is allowed, but No Satellite Dishes.
No Washing Machine or Dryer Allowed

Owner will check Income, Landlord References, Credit, Eviction History, and Criminal History.
Family Interview Required.

Unit Ready for Occupancy on April 1st
Rent: $800

Security Deposit of $800 Required in Advance with First Month's Rent

Call Owner at: 222-555-1234

Questions: Would you want to live here? Would you go to look at the apartment?

EXHIBIT 2[26]

From HUD Handbook 4350.3 CHG-24

FIGURE 2-4

**EXAMPLES OF PROHIBITED ACTIONS
OWNERS AND THEIR REPRESENTATIVES ARE
PROHIBITED FROM:**

o Following policies that subject qualified individuals with handicaps to discrimination on the basis of handicap. (504 and FH Act)

o Denying a unit to an otherwise qualified applicant because of a handicap of that renter or a person residing or intending to reside in that dwelling after it is rented. (504 and FH Act)

o Denying an otherwise qualified individual with handicaps the equal opportunity to participate in and receive and enjoy the benefits of tenancy and any services provided. (504 and FH Act)

o Providing any housing services, aids, and benefits that are not as effective in affording the qualified individual with handicaps an equal opportunity to obtain the same result, to gain the same benefit or reach the same level of achievement as provided

[26] http://www.hudclips.org

others. While the owner is not required to provide services, if they decide to provide services, this statement applies. (504 and FH Act)

o   Providing different or separate housing, services, aids, and benefits to either an individual or class of individuals with handicaps unless such action is necessary to provide services that are as effective as those provided others. (504 and FH Act)

o   Denying a qualified individual with handicaps the opportunity to participate as a member of planning or advisory boards. (504)

o   Preventing a tenant from using assistive devices, auxiliary alarms or guides. (504 and FH Act)

EXHIBIT 3

Date: _____

_____ (Rental Applicant)

_____

_____

_____

Permission to Release Information

I authorize the ☐ Owner ☐ Broker ☐ Management Agent, _____, mailing address _____ state: _____, zip code: _____ to obtain whatever information considered necessary and legal under the laws of the State of _____ in order to process my rental application.

I further grant permission for the Owner, Broker or Management Agent to obtain verification information, such as a credit check, landlord check, eviction and criminal history reports, employment, income and bank account verification information, and any other information allowed under the law.

I understand that my credit report may be accessed now and in the future in order to obtain information, and/or to submit information regarding past, current, and future tenancies. The person(s) and/or agencies handling my rental application will hold this information in confidence.

I understand that these reports are necessary in order to process my rental application, to report and/or obtain information regarding tenancy status, and/or in order to comply with city, state, municipal, or federal government regulations, ordinances, subsidies, policies or procedures.

I understand that I am not assured an apartment on the basis of permitting the release of this information. It is a means to process, confirm and verify my rental application information for consideration and reporting purposes only.

_____   _____

Applicant / Tenant / Co-Signer   Social Security #

Date: _____ Telephone: (_____)

_____

Owner/Manager/Agent/Broker

Date: _____ Telephone: (_____) _____

cc: File

Attorney: _____

Carolyn Gibson

<u>EXHIBIT 4</u>

Application Processing Form

<u>This form must be completed before any application is approved.</u>

DATE OF APPLICATION: _____**2003**
PERSON PROCESSING:_____

Address of Apt: _____
BR SIZE:_____

APPLICANT NAME(S):_____
& _____

ADDRESS: _____
APT. #_____   PHONE: (_____)_____

CITY: _____
STATE: _____   ZIP CODE:_____

WHAT IS NEEDED	DATE MAILED	WHEN RETURNED
__PHOTO IDENTIFICATION OF HEAD	_____	_____
__INTERVIEW WITH APPLICANT	_____	_____
__REQUEST FOR ADD'L INFORMATION	_____	_____
__LANDLORD VERIFICATION: _____	_____	_____
__LANDLORD VERIFICATION: _____	_____	_____
__LANDLORD VERIFICATION: _____	_____	_____
__EMPLOYMENT VERIFICATION:____	_____	_____
__EMPLOYMENT VERIFICATION:____	_____	_____
__EMPLOYMENT VERIFICATION:____	_____	_____
__AFDC VERIFICATION: _____	_____	_____
__AFDC VERIFICATION: _____	_____	_____
__DISABILITY/PENSION: _____	_____	_____
__UNEMPLOYMENT VERIFICATION	_____	_____
__SOCIAL SECURITY: _____	_____	_____
__SSI VERIFICATION: _____	_____	_____
__VETERANS BENEFITS: ____	_____	_____
__ALIMONY INCOME	_____	_____
__CHILD SUPPORT INCOME	_____	_____
__UNEMPLOYMENT INCOME	_____	_____
__SOCIAL SECURITY CARD_____	_____	_____
__SOCIAL SECURITY CARD_____	_____	_____
__SOCIAL SECURITY CARD_____	_____	_____
__SOCIAL SECURITY CARD_____	_____	_____
__SOCIAL SECURITY CARD_____	_____	_____
__CREDIT CHECK #1 _____	_____	_____
__CREDIT CHECK #2 _____	_____	_____
__CREDIT CHECK #3 _____	_____	_____
__CREDIT CHECK #4 _____	_____	_____
__NO INCOME CERTIFICATION #2 _____	_____	
__HEALTH BENEFIT'S VERIFICATION	_____	_____
__HANDICAP VERIFICATION	_____	_____
__FULL TIME STUDENT VERIF.: ____	_____	_____
__FULL TIME STUDENT VERIF.____	_____	_____
__NO INCOME CERTIFICATION #1	_____	_____

Carolyn Gibson

VERIFICATIONS NEEDED NAME	**DATE MAILED**	**WHEN RETURNED**
__BIRTH CERTIFICATE #1 _____	_____	_____
__BIRTH CERTIFICATE #2 _____	_____	_____
__BIRTH CERTIFICATE #3 _____	_____	_____
__BIRTH CERTIFICATE #4 _____	_____	_____
__BIRTH CERTIFICATE #5 _____	_____	_____
__BIRTH CERTIFICATE #6 _____	_____	_____
__BIRTH CERTIFICATE #7 _____	_____	_____
__CHILD CARE VERIFICATION	_____	_____
__BANK ACCOUNT VERIFICATION	_____	_____
__BANK ACCOUNT VERIFICATION	_____	_____
__CERTIFICATE OF DEPOSIT	_____	_____
__SECTION 8 CERTIFICATE	_____	_____
__SECTION 8 VOUCHER	_____	_____
__CORI[27] CHECK FOR _____	_____	_____
__CORI CHECK FOR _____	_____	_____
__CORI CHECK FOR _____	_____	_____
__CORI CHECK FOR _____	_____	_____
__CORI CHECK FOR _____	_____	_____

****

Application Status: ☐ APPROVED ☐ NOT APPROVED
By: _____

Applicant informed of Rejection/Non-Selection On:
_____, 2003   By: _____

Application Withdrawn by Applicant On: _____, 2003
By: ☐ Telephone ☐ In Person ☐ By Letter ☐ By email

Reason for The Withdrawal: _____

Comments: _____

---

[27] CORI = Criminal Offender Registration Information 6/03

EXHIBIT 5
Apartment Inspection Form

APARTMENT INSPECTION FORM				Type of Inspection:
Name of Occupant:				Date of Inspection: _____, 2000
Address:			Apt.:	# of Bedrooms:

	Tenant	Owner		
Refrigerator Belongs To:			Stove is: _____ Gas _____ Electric	
				Comments
Insects? Mice?	Yes	No		
# of Smoke Detectors ____ Working? Batteries Needed? Wires Loose?	Yes	No		

RECEPTION AREA	Pass	Fail	Tenant Damage	Comments
Condition of Ceiling				
Condition of Walls				
Condition of Floor				
Condition of Ceiling Light Fixture				
Condition of Wall Outlets				
Condition of Windows & Screens				
Baseboard Heat				

MASTER BEDROOM	Pass	Fail	Tenant Damage	Comments
Condition of Ceiling				
Condition of Walls				
Condition of Floor				
Light Fixture on Ceiling				
Condition of Wall Outlets				
Light Fixture on Wall(s)				
Condition of Windows & Screens				
Baseboard Heat				
Condition of Doors				

BEDROOM TWO	Pass	Fail	Tenant Damage	Comments
Condition of Ceiling				
Condition of Walls				
Condition of Floor				
Light Fixture on Ceiling				
Condition of Wall Outlets				
Light Fixture of Wall(s)				
Windows				
Window Screens				
Window Shades				
Baseboard Heat				
Condition of Doors				

BEDROOM THREE	Pass	Fail	Tenant Damage	Comments
Condition of Ceiling				
Condition of Walls				
Condition of Floor				
Light Fixture on Ceiling				
Condition of Wall Outlets				
Light Fixture on Wall(s)				
Condition of Windows				
Window Screens				
Window Shades				
Baseboard Heat				
Condition of Doors				

Apartment Inspection Form

PAGE 2	Pass	Fail	Tenant Damage	Comments
KITCHEN				
Condition of Ceiling				
Condition of Walls				
Condition of Floor				
Upper Cabinets				
Lower Cabinets				
Fire Extinguisher on Wall				
Condition of Stove				
Refrigerator Condition				
Light Fixtures & Outlets				
Wall Fixtures				
Condition of Pantry				
Condition of Sink				
Garbage Disposal				
	Pass	Fail	Tenant Damage	Comments
LIVING ROOM				
Condition of Ceiling				
Condition of Walls				
Condition of Floor				
Light Fixture on Ceiling				
Condition of Wall Outlets				
Light Fixture on Wall(s)				
Condition of Windows & Screens				
Heat Thermostat				
Baseboard Heat				
Condition of Doors				
	Pass	Fail	Tenant Damage	Comments
BATHROOM				
Condition of Ceiling				
Condition of Walls				
Condition of Wall Outlet/GFI Switch				
Condition of Floor				
Condition of Bath Tub & Pop-Up				
Shower/Head - Any Leak?				
Shower Curtain Rod				
Is There a Shower Curtain?				
Medicine Cabinet/Inside				
Condition of Window/ Screens				
Window Shade Condition				
Soap Holder				
Tooth Brush Holder				
Condition of Toilet (Any Leaks?)				
Condition of Toilet Seat				
Condition of Sink & Pop-Up				
Condition of Ceiling Fan - Clean?				
Baseboard Heat				
Condition of Door				
General Comments				**General Comments**

Date of Last Painting: _____

General Housekeeping Comments _____

Inspection By: _____ Title: _____

Tenant Signature: _____ Date: _____, 2000

Work Orders Made Up: _____, 2000

EXHIBIT 6

Landlord Verification

To:_____   Date: _____

_____

_____

_____

Dear Mr./Ms._____:

_____, is ☐ Currently Living ☐ Formerly Lived at _____Apt. _____ in _____ and gave us your name and address as the ☐ Present ☐ Former Landlord. This rental applicant is looking to rent from us. In order that we may make a determination regarding his/her qualifications as a possible tenant, we would appreciate your answering the following questions and returning this form to us in the enclosed envelope. **This information will be kept confidential**. We will not divulge what is written on this form to the tenant.

I give permission to _____ to request the information requested below for the purpose of determining my qualifications as a rental applicant. I understand that what is written in response will be held in confidence, and that the person(s) requesting the information will not tell me what was written on the form.

_____ Date: _____

Carolyn Gibson

Rental Applicant Signature

Was the apartment in the applicant's name above? ☐Yes ☐ No
If no, who did/does the apartment belong to? _____

How long did the tenant live there?   From: _____ to _____

How many people occupied the apartment?
_____ Adults _____ Children under 18 years old

How much is or was the rent? $ _____ per _____

How much was the security deposit collected? $ _____

Did the tenant have a written lease?   ☐Yes   ☐ No

Did he or she stay until the full term of the lease? ☐Yes   ☐ No

Did the tenant pay the rent on time?   ☐Yes   ☐ No

Does the tenant still owe you rent money?   ☐Yes $ ___ ☐ No
Did you ever have to send the applicant an eviction notice?

              ☐Yes   ☐ No
For non-payment of rent? If yes, how many times? _____

Does the tenant still owe you damage money? ☐Yes $___ ☐ No
Did/Does the tenant have a pet? How Many? _____

              ☐Yes   ☐ No

Did/Does the tenant have a washing machine/dryer? ☐Yes ☐ No
Any complaints about the applicant from other tenants?

              ☐Yes   ☐ No
If yes, please explain:

_____

Why did the tenant move out? Why is the tenant moving out? ___

_____

The tenant left your apartment in

☐ Excellent ☐ Good ☐ Poor Condition

Would you rent an apartment to this tenant again? ☐ Yes ☐ No

Any final comments you would like to make not mentioned here?

_____

_____

****

I am the ☐ Homeowner ☐ Landlord ☐ Management Agent

☐ Manager for the above listed property. I have provided the above information as truthful to the best of my ability.

_____ Date: _____

Homeowner/Manager/Agent
Telephone Number (_____) _____

Thank you for your honesty and cooperation in completing this form

Please make a copy of this form for your own records and return it to:

_____   _____

_____   _____

    Telephone: (_____)   _____

PLEASE <u>DO NOT</u> GIVE THIS FORM TO YOUR CURRENT OR FORMER TENANT TO GIVE TO US!!!!!

EXHIBIT 7

Employment Verification Form

To:_____   Date: _____

_____

_____

_____   **Human Resource Department**

Dear _____:

_____, is currently living at
_____ Apt. _____ in
_____ and gave us your name and
address as the current place of employment.

Your employee is looking to rent from us. In order that we may
make a determination regarding his/her financial qualifications as
a possible tenant, we would appreciate your answering the
following questions and returning this form to us in the enclosed
envelope **The information received will be kept confidential** in
the rental applicant's file. We will not divulge what is written on
this form to the tenant. Its only purpose is to confirm current
and/or continued eligibility for a rental unit.

Employee Name: _____ Job Title: _____

How long has the employee worked here? Since: _____

At What Base Rate of Pay?

☐ Annual $ _____ ☐ Bi-Weekly $ _____

Carolyn Gibson

As of what date? _____

       ☐ Weekly $ _____ ☐ Per Hour $ _____

What is the average number of hours worked per week at base rate? _____

Overtime Pay Rate: $ _____ per hour

Average number of overtime hours worked per week: $ _____

Bonus Compensation?

       ☐ Yes   ☐ No   Amount $ _____   Per _____

Vacation Pay?

       ☐ Yes   ☐ No   Amount $ _____   Per _____

Does Employee receive any other form of compensation?

                                         ☐ Yes   ☐ No

Please Specify: _____

_____

Possibility of Future Employment: _____

I give permission to _____ to have the information requested for the purpose of determining my financial qualifications as a rental applicant. I understand that what is written in response will be held in confidence.

_____ Date: _____
Rental Applicant Signature

****

Name of Company: _____

Authorized Person Completing This Form: _____

Title: _____

Telephone # (_____) _____ Ext. _____

**Thank You for taking the time to complete this form.
Please make a copy of this form for your own records
and return it to:**

_____ Title _____

_____ _____

_____
Telephone # (_____) _____

PLEASE <u>DO NOT</u> GIVE THIS FORM
TO YOUR EMPLOYEE TO GIVE TO US!!!!!

__Index__

Carolyn Gibson

About the Author

Carolyn Gibson, CPM® is president of Synergy Professional Services in Boston, Massachusetts. She is a veteran property manager and consultant in the management, marketing, staff training, and leasing of residential, nonprofit, and government-assisted properties.

Ms. Gibson holds the Certified Property Manager® designation from the Chicago based Institute of Real Estate Management®, and is a member of their national faculty.

She has been published in the *Journal of Property Management (JPM),* and the *New England Real Estate Journal,* and featured in *The Boston Globe and Boston Herald* newspapers.

Carolyn is a graduate of Simmons College in Boston, Massachusetts.